About the Authors

In the course of their careers in the business of writing and selling books, RUSSELL ASH and BRIAN LAKE have collected hundreds of bizarre examples from this extensive field. From double entendres and astonishingly specialized subjects to weird books on horticulture, science, and medical matters, the authors have left no catalog page unturned in their quest for the most bizarre of books.

FISH WHO ANSWER
THE TELEPHONE
and other studies in experimental biology

by Professor Y. FROLOV

With a Preface by ELEANOR GRAHAM

BIZARRE BOOKS

A COMPENDIUM OF CLASSIC ODDITIES

RUSSELL ASH and BRIAN LAKE

HARPER PERENNIAL

NEW YORK • LONDON • TORONTO • SYDNEY

HARPER ● PERENNIAL

First published in Great Britain in 2006
under the title *Fish Who Answer the Telephone* by
John Murray (Publishers), a division of Hodder Headline.

HarperCollins books may be purchased for educational, business, or sales
promotional use. For information please write: Special Markets Department,
HarperCollins Publishers, 10 East 53rd Street, New York, NY 10022.

FIRST U.S. EDITION

Library of Congress Cataloging-in-Publication Data has been applied for.

ISBN: 978-0-06-134665-1
ISBN-10: 0-06-134665-9

07 08 09 10 11 RRD 10 9 8 7 6 5 4 3 2 1

CONTENTS

INTRODUCTION

This is the pick of the crop of Bizarre Books.

With forty-plus years' joint experience of scouring bookshops, bookfairs, publishers' lists, book trade periodicals and internet sites, the compilers can claim a certain limited expertise in the subject.

There are hundreds of titles in *Fish Who Answer the Telephone* selected from thousands more which remain undisturbed in dusty libraries, waiting for the publication of the authors' ultimate fantasy retirement project, *The Complete Bizarre Books*. Meanwhile, this is the *crème de la crème*.

Branko Bokun's *Humour Therapy*, 1986 (see page 94) – don't laugh, it cured Norman Cousins of cancer – tries to answer the old question 'What is laughter?'. Mr Bokun mentions 'incongruity theories' – laughter caused by 'unusual, inconsistent or incompatible pairing of ideas, situations, behaviour or attitudes'. 'Authors and titles' might have been added to his list, just for instance, *The Lord's Supper* by William Ovens, or David Blot's *Put It In Writing*.

All the books recorded are *real* titles, with *real* authors. All of them were published with the serious intention of informing, not amusing. In this they have signally failed.

Titles that tell a different story from that originally intended set our scene – *Flashes from the Welsh Pulpit* and *Drummer Dick's Discharge* are from another age, almost another language.

Most of the other sections are loosely divided by subject, the books ranging from the obviously mad and instantly funny through to the outwardly innocuous but inwardly very weird indeed.

We conclude with some books that have been published 'against all odds'; as Gilbert Anderson wrote in 1993, *There Must be a Reason* – but the answer is not obvious.

Without our many researchers in libraries, the book trade, collectors and enthusiasts worldwide, this collection would be a shadow of its current glory and we thank them profusely; their names are listed on pages 216–17. We would like to thank the following for particular help in the preparation of *Fish Who Answer the Telephone*: Robin Summers, Raymond Briggs, Tony Barrett and, for the more cerebrally challenging entries, Eric Korn.

Bizarre Books as a genre won't stop here – keep 'em coming!

Brian Lake
books@jarndyce.co.uk

Russell Ash
ash@pavilion.co.uk

NOTES

All books are published in London unless otherwise stated.
Most chapters are arranged alphabetically by author.
n.d.: no date
n.p.: no publisher

1
DOUBLE ENTENDRE
They didn't really mean it

The Resistance of Piles to Penetration
Russell V. Allin
Spon, 1935

Games You Can Play with Your Pussy
Ira Alterman
Watertown, Mass.: Ivory Tower Pub. Co., 1985

The Boy Fancier
Frank Townend Barton
Routledge; New York: E. P. Dutton, 1912

Enter Ye In
James Sidlow Baxter
Edinburgh: Marshall, Morgan & Scott, 1939

Having entered, Baxter later wrote:
Going Deeper
Edinburgh: Marshall, Morgan & Scott, 1960

The Last Agony of the Great Bore
F. W. Bird
Boston, Mass.: Dutton, 1868
On the drilling of the Hoosac Tunnel.

The Line of Cleavage Under Elizabeth
Dom Norbert Birt
Catholic Truth Society, 1909

Enid Blyton's Gay Story Book
Enid Blyton
Hodder & Stoughton, 1946

The stories include:
Let's Play Worms
Dame Poke-Around
Her other popular tales include:
Mr Pink-Whistle Interferes
A Rubbalong Tale
Noddy Loses His Clothes
Ticklem-Up the Gnome
Dame Slap and Her School

Camp Contact
Edward Newbold Bradley
Thomas Nelson, 1941

Benjamin Holt's Boys and What they did for him
Ellen Brook
S. W. Partridge, 1881

Foch Talks
Cdt Bugnet
Victor Gollancz, 1929

A Glowing and Graphic Description of the Great Hole
Mrs D. U. C.
Syracuse, NY: Daily Democrat Office, 1848

Miss Rod. The Girl's Own Book
Mme Camerlynck-Guernier
Paris: H. Didier, 1934

'Dear Miss Rod, Having heard much about you, your cheerful temper, and clever way of nursing, through our mutual friend Dr Garrett, I long to have you come and nurse me . . . Dr Garrett is going to write to you about the business part of the question.'

FOCH
TALKS

by
Commandant
Bugnet,
aide-de-camp
to Foch,
1921 - 1929

Queer Shipmates
Archibald Bruce Campbell
Phoenix House, 1962

Old Dykes I Have Known
P. R. Charnley
Grantham: Barney Books, 1996

Single-Handed Cruising
Francis Bernard Cooke
Edward Arnold, 1919

Some Account of my Intercourse with Madame Blavatsky from 1872 to 1884
Emma Coulomb
Elliot Stock, 1885

Shag the Pony
Peter Crabbe
Catholic Truth Society, 1952

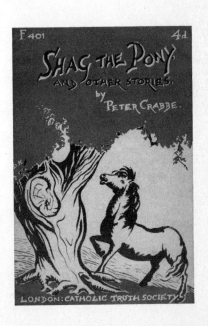

Five Years Hard
Frank Percy Crozier
New York: J. Cape & R. Ballou, 1932

Flashes from the Welsh Pulpit
J. Gwnoro Davies (ed.)
Hodder & Stoughton, 1889

> ' . . . it is to be hoped that these Flashes have retained sufficient *heat* to warm some Christian's heart.'

The Boy Hunter
Colin Day
Blackie & Son, 1938

Drummer Dick's Discharge
Beatrix M. De Burgh
Ernest Nister, 1902

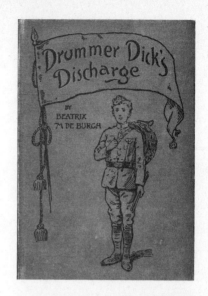

Penetrating Wagner's Ring
John Louis DiGaetani
*Rutherford, NJ: Fairleigh Dickinson
University Press, 1978*

Queer Chums
Charles Henry Eden
S.P.C.K., 1887

Fishing for Boys
J. H. Elliott
George G. Harrap, 1961

Girls Who Did
Helen Josephine Ferris
New York: E. P. Dutton, c.1927

Fanny at School
Frances Dana Gage
Buffalo, NY: Breed, Butler & Co., 1866

Erections on Allotments
George W. Giles and Fred M.
Osborn
Central Allotments Committee, n.d.

Whippings and Lashings
The Girl Guides Association, 1977

Cock Tugs

W. B. Hallam

Liverpool: Printed by James Birchall & Sons, 1963

'A Short History of the Liverpool Screw Towing Company'

Kept for the Master's Use

F. R. Havergal

J. Nisbet, 1879

Newly Discovered French Letters

Richmond Laurin Hawkins

Cambridge, MA: Harvard University Press, 1933

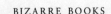

Big Dick, the King of the Negroes

Harry Hazel [pseudonym of Justin Jones]

Boston, MA: Star Spangled Banner Office, 1846

'Or, Virtue and Vice Contrasted. A Romance of High & Low Life in Boston.'

Boobs as Seen by John Henry

George Vere Hobart

New York: G. W. Dillingham, 1914

Dick's Fairy

Silas Kitto Hocking

Warne & Co., 1883

'A Tale of the Streets and Other Stories'

Men Who Have Risen: A Book for Boys

J. Hogg (ed.)

J. Hogg & Sons, 1859

MEN WHO HAVE RISEN

A BOOK FOR BOYS

ILLUSTRATED BY C. A. DOYLE

LONDON · J · HOGG · AND · SONS
AND · EDINBURGH ·

Handbook for the Limbless
Geoffrey Howson (ed.)
Disabled Society, 1922
With a foreword by John Galsworthy.

The Nature and Tendency of Balls, Seriously and Candidly Considered in Two Sermons
Jacob Ide
Dedham, 1818

The Chronicles of the Crutch
Blanchard Jerrold
William Tinsley, 1860

Microscopic Objects: How to Mount Them
Jean C. Johnson
English Universities Press, 1948

In and Out of Florence
Vernon Lyman Kellogg
New York: Holt, 1910

The Big Problem of Small Organs
Alan T. Kitley
Colchester: The Author, 1966

> ' Having spent ten years devising schemes for the small organ I reluctantly decided that "there ain't no such animal", as a famous cowboy once said.'

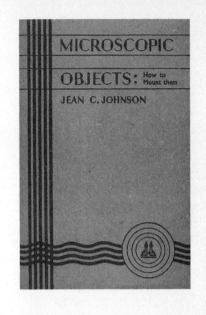

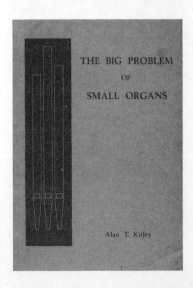

Explorations at Sodom
Melvin Grove Kyle
Religious Tract Society, 1928

Memorable Balls
James Laver
Derek Verschoyle, 1954

Briefs Calmly Considered
'A Layman'
York: A. Barclay, 1826

Shifts and Expedients of Camp Life
William Barry Lord and Thomas Baines
Horace Cox, 1871

The Midnight Cry; or, Signs in the Church of the Bridegroom's Second Coming
Rev. J. Lowes
Carlisle: n.p., 1800

> ' Fire from Heaven . . . has burnt up our natural *heavens* of joy and delight in the flesh.'

Joyful Lays
Rev. R. Lowry and W. Howard Doane
New York and Chicago: Biglow & Main, 1886

Cock Angel
Rachel Swete Macnamara
Hurst & Blackett, 1928

Queer Doings in the Navy
Asa M. Mattice
Cambridge, MA: Line Officers' Association, 1896

BRIEFS

CALMLY CONSIDERED.

BY A LAYMAN.

Audi alteram partem.

YORK:
PUBLISHED BY A. BARCLAY,
AND SOLD BY C. AND J. RIVINGTON, J. HATCHARD AND SON,
AND L. B. SEELEY AND SON, LONDON.

1826.

Two Men Came Together
Roy McCarthy
Derby: Rolls-Royce Ltd, 1954

School Experiences of a Fag at a Private and a Public School
George Melly
Smith, Elder & Co., 1854

Ay, Ay, Hev Ye a Spunk?
William A. Mutch
Dundee: J. Leng & Co., 1918

Cobbler's Knob
Eleanore Myers
Dennis Dobson, 1958

Draw In Your Stool
Oliver Onions
Mills & Boon, 1909

A Love Passage
Lady Harriet Phillimore
Christian Knowledge Society, 1908

Scouts in Bondage
Geoffrey Prout
Aldine Publishing Co., 1930

'Stories of stern endeavour are always interesting as well as elevating . . . The scouts in this story, though fettered for a while by a period of bondage, are just the jolly, good-natured, determined boys who are typical of a country troop . . . And what a stirring series of adventures and mysterious experiences they all had . . . '

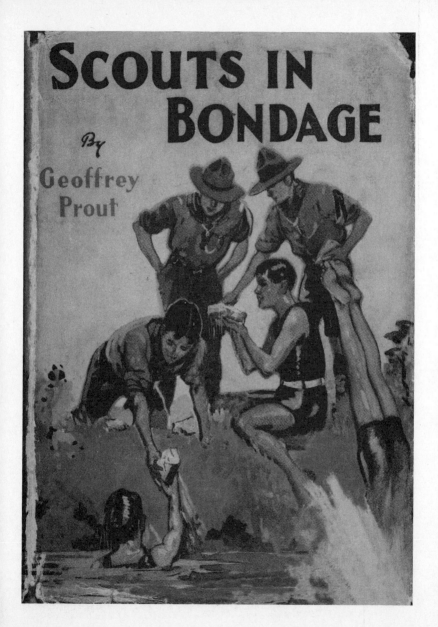

SCOUTS IN BONDAGE

By Geoffrey Prout

Prout was also the author of:

Trawler Boy Dick
C. A. Pearson, 1927

Chats on Big and Little Fiddles
Olga Racster
T. Werner Laurie, 1924

The Little Horn's Doom & Downfall
Mary Rande
Printed for the Author, 1651

Report of the Committee on Relations with Junior Members
Oxford: Oxford University Gazette, 1963

Shag the Caribou
Cecil Bernard Rutley
Macmillan, 1941

'For all important purposes, this is a true story.' *It was published with Rutley's* Frisk the Otter *and* Gogo the Penguin.

The Randy
and
Fairies on the Doorstep
Dorothy Sanders
Sydney: Australian Publishing Co., 1948

Under Two Queens
John Huntley Skrine
Macmillan, 1884

SHAG
THE CARIBOU

The Scrubber Strategy
Robert T. Stafford
New York: Harper & Row, 1982

The Queer Side of Landlordism
J. F. Sullivan
The English Land Restoration League, 1892

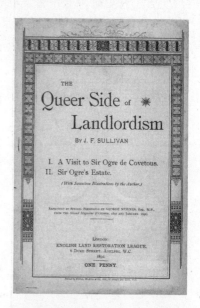

'English Land Restoration League. Object: The Abolition of Landlordism. Method: The abolition of all taxes upon labour and the products of labour and the earnings of labour and the increase of taxation upon land values until the whole annual value of land is taken in taxation for public purposes.'

Girls of the Pansy Patrol
May Wynne
Aldine Publishing Co., 1931

'The girls of the Pansy Patrol were lucky in having a Guider who loved and understood them. As to the camping ground, I venture to think that every Girl Guide will be wanting one like it, once she has read of the adventures which befell Jessamy and her chums. '

The Big Book of Busts
John L. Watson
San Francisco, CA: Hypermodern Press, 1994

The Gay Boys of Old Yale!
John Denison Vose
New Haven, CT: Hunter & Co., c.1869

Invisible Dick
Frank Topham
D. C. Thomson & Co., 1926

'"Jeehosophat! What a disgraceful scene!" said Dick Brett, doing a series of physical jerks behind a bush, as he began to grow into visibility.'

Organ Building for Amateurs
Mark Wicks
Ward Lock, 1887

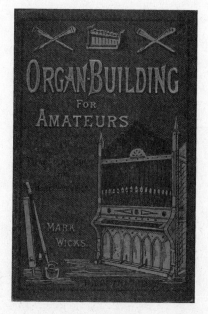

'The perseverance devoted to building even a small organ at home must necessarily afford most valuable training to young men, and the moral value of the instrument itself . . . cannot, I think, be over-estimated.'

A Three-Foot Stool
Peter Wright
Smith, Elder & Co., 1909

2

AUTHORS – RIGHT OR WRONG

Jane Arbor
The Cypress Garden
Mills & Boon, 1969

Michael Armacost
The Politics of Weapons Innovation
New York: Columbia University Press, 1969

I. Atack
The Ethics of Peace and War
Edinburgh: Edinburgh University Press, 2005

Aaron H. Axelrod
Machine Tool Operation
New York: McGraw-Hill, 1941

Earl R. Babble
The Practice of Social Research
Wadsworth, 1975

Canon Ball
The Voyage of Life
S.P.C.K., 1915

Claude Balls
Shy Men, Sex, and Castrating Women
Trexlertown, PA: Polemic Press, 1985

Michael Balls
Organ Culture in Biomedical Research
Cambridge: Cambridge University Press, 1976

Mrs M. A. Banger
Lead the Way Ladies!
Brighton: Brighton Herald, 1906

Robin Banks
Punishment
Harmondsworth: Penguin, 1972

William Battie
A Treatise on Madness
J. Whiston & B. White, 1758

'Madness is frequently taken for one species of disorder, nevertheless, when thoroughly examined, it discovers as much variety with respect to its causes and circumstances as any distemper whatever: Madness, therefore, like most other morbid cases, rejects all general methods, e.g. bleeding, blisters, caustics, rough cathartics, the gums and faetid anti-hysterics, opium, mineral waters, cold bathings and vomits.'
Not quite so batty after all . . .

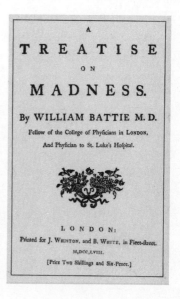

A
TREATISE
ON
MADNESS.

By WILLIAM BATTIE M. D.
Fellow of the College of Phyſicians in LONDON,
And Phyſician to St. Luke's Hoſpital.

LONDON:
Printed for J. WHISTON, and B. WHITE, in Fleet-ſtreet.
M,DCC,LVIII.
[Price Two Shillings and Six-Pence.]

Jack Kenneth Bellchambers
Devonshire Clockmakers
Totnes: The Author, 1962

Stephen E. Beltz
How to Make Johnny Want to Obey
Englewood Cliffs, NJ: Prentice-Hall, 1971

Superintendent James Bent ➤
Criminal Life: Reminiscences of Forty-Two Years as a Police Officer
Manchester: John Heywood, 1891

Herbert Roderick Bird
Farm Poultry Raising
Washington, DC: United States Department of Agriculture, 1948

David Blot
Put it in Writing
Rowley, MA: Newbury House Publishers, 1980

Walter Russell Brain (Baron Brain)
Diseases of the Nervous System
Oxford: Oxford University Press, 1933

Mary Breasted
Oh! Sex Education!
New York: Praeger Publishers, 1970

Clara Louise Burnham
The Inner Flame
Constable, 1912

Raymond Bush
Fruit Growing Outdoors
Faber & Faber, 1946

Geoff Carless
Motorcycling for Beginners
East Ardsley: EP Publishing, 1980

Nonce Casanova
La Libertine
Amiens: E. Malfère, 1921

W. Chappell
The Preacher; or, The Art and Method of Preaching
Edward Farnham, 1656

Yours truly

James Burt

John Chipping
Your Teeth
Cottrell & Co., 1967

Edward H. Clinkscale
A Musical Offering
New York: Pendragon Press, 1977

Douglas J. Cock
Every Other Inch a Methodist
Epworth Press, 1987

William Cockburn
The Symptoms, Nature, Cause, and Cure of a [*sic*] Gonorrhoea
G. Strahan, 1713

Margaret Coffin
Death in Early America: The History and Folklore of Customs
and Superstitions of Early Medicine, Funerals, Burial and
Mournings
New York: E. P. Dutton, 1976

Nicholas Cox, preface by E. D. Cuming
The Gentleman's Recreation
Cresset Press, 1928

A. Dick
Inside Story
Allen & Unwin, 1943

Emerson and Russell Dobash
Violence Against Wives
Shepton Mallet: Open Books, 1980

Dr Stretch Dowse
A Primer of the Art of Massage (For Learners)
Bristol: John Wright & Sons, 1892, 8th edition, illustrated

Raymond W. Dull
Mathematics for Engineers
New York: McGraw-Hill Book Company, 1926, 2nd edition 1941

Peter Elbow
Writing with Power
Oxford: Oxford University Press, 1981

George Fasting
How to Live to a Hundred Years or More
New York: The Author, 1927

Frank Finn
The Boy's Own Aquarium
Country Life *and George Newnes, 1922*

Eric Fuchs
Sexual Desire and Love
Cambridge: J. Clarke, 1983

Sir Wilmot Hudson Fysh
Round the Bend in the Stream
Sydney: Angus & Robertson, 1968

Rev. Joseph Gay
Common Truths from Queer Texts
Arthur Stockwell, 1908

Paul J. Gillette
Vasectomy: The Male Sterilization Operation
New York: Paperback Library, 1972

P. V. Glob
The Bog People
Faber & Faber, 1969

Maurice Golesworthy
The Encyclopaedia of Association Football
Robert Hale, 1967

John Goodbody
Illustrated History of Gymnastics
Stanley Paul, 1983

Paula Gosling
A Running Duck
Pan Books, 1979

Roger Grounds
The Perfect Lawn
Ward Lock, 1974

Anita Hardon
Monitoring Family Planning & Reproductive Rights
New York: WHAF, 1997

Paula Hardwick
Discovering Horn
Lutterworth, 1981

Leo Heaps
The High Rise
W. H. Allen, 1972

Robin Hood
Industrial Social Security in the South
Chapel Hill, NC: The University of North Carolina Press, 1936

Karen Horney
The Adolescent Diaries
New York: Basic Books, 1980

Benjamin Humpage
An Essay on the Rupture called Hydrocele
John Murray, 1788

Norman Knight
Chess Pieces
Sutton Coldfield: Chess, 1968

Captain John Knott
Lashing and Securing of Deck Cargoes
Nautical Institute, 1994

Morris Krok
From the Deathbed to Boisterous Health
Durban: Essence of Health, 1963

Louis Lasagna
Obesity: Causes, Consequences, and Treatment
New York: Medcom Press, 1974

John Leak (translator)
New and Rare Inventions of Water-Works
Joseph Moxon, 1659

H. W. A. Linecar
British Electric Trains
Ian Allan, 1947

Leslie Lines
Solid Geometry
Macmillan & Co., 1935

William W. Looney
Anatomy of the Brain
Philadelphia, PA: F. A. Davis, 2nd edition, 1932

A. Lord
The Grace of God
Truro: James R. Netherton, 1859

G. A. Martini
Metabolic Changes Induced by Alcohol
Berlin: Springer-Verlag, 1971

Anna Mews
Care for Your Kitten
Collins, 1986

L. G. Chiozza Money
Riches and Poverty
Methuen, 1905

Anthony Netboy
Salmon: The World's Most Harassed Fish
Tulsa, OK: Winchester Press, 1980

Kenneth Neil Ogle
Researches in Binocular Vision
Philadelphia, PA: W. B. Saunders, 1950

William Gilbert Ovens
The Lord's Supper
Church Association, 1940

Rev. E. I. D. Pepper
Spices from the Lord's Garden
West Conshohocken, PA: n.p., 1895

C. C. Pounder
Marine Diesel Engines
George Newnes, 1952

Brian Pronger
The Arena of Masculinity: Sports, Homosexuality,
and the Meaning of Sex
New York: St. Martin's Press, 1990

Helmut Puff
Sodomy in Reformation Germany and Switzerland, 1400–1600
Chicago: University of Chicago Press, 2003

Dan G. Pursuit, et al
Police Programs for Preventing Crime and Delinquency
Springfield, IL: Charles C. Thomas, 1972

J. H. Quilter
The Trimming and Finishing of Hosiery and Hosiery Fabrics
Bradford: C. Greening, 1889

Walter Cade Reckless
The Prevention of Juvenile
Delinquency
*Columbus, OH: Ohio State University
Press, 1972*

George Robb
White-Collar Crime in Modern
England
*Cambridge: Cambridge University
Press, 1992*

William Sinker
By Reef and Shoal
Christian Knowledge Society, 1904

John Skull
Speak Your Mind
Hart-Davis, 1969

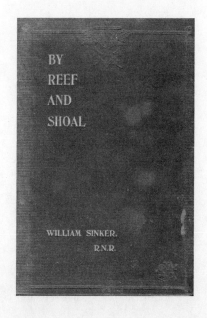

Silken Threads

by
Wilhelmina Stitch

Methuen & Co. Ltd.
London

One Shilling and Threepence net

Frank Gill Slaughter
Lifeblood
New York: Doubleday, 1974
Slaughter was also the author of **That None Shall Die** *(Jarrold, 1942).*

Robert Smellie
The Skipper's Secret
Edinburgh: D. M. Small, 1898

Daniel Snowman
Frozen Future: The Arctic, the Antarctic and the Survival of the Planet
Toronto: Random House of Canada, 1993

R. Solow
Price Expectations and the Behaviour of the Price Level
Manchester: Manchester University Press, 1970

Bang-Song Song
Korean Music
Seoul: Jimoondang Publishing Co., 2000

R. A. Sparkes
Electronics for Schools
Hutchinson Educational, 1972

Wilhelmina Stitch
Silken Threads
Methuen & Co., 1927, 16th edition, 1942

Jack Roy Strange
Abnormal Psychology: Understanding Behavior Disorders
New York: McGraw-Hill, 1965

Adrienne P. Swindells
Crime and Law
Hart-Davis, 1977
Swindells was also the author of **Running a Disco, Drugs** *and*
Throwing a Party *(all Hart-Davis, 1978).*

Désiré Tits
La Formation de la Jeunesse
Bruxelles: Office de Publicité, 1945

Mary Twelveponies
There Are No Problem Horses, Only Problem Riders
Boston, MA: Houghton Mifflin, 1982

Richard P. Vine
Winemaking: From Grape Growing to Marketplace
New York: Chapman & Hall, 1997

Guysbert B. Vroom
Fuel Oil Viscosity-Temperature Diagram
New York: Simmons-Boardman, 1926

Lloyd T. Walker
The Biomechanics of the Human Foot
Glasgow: University of Strathclyde, 1991

Sir Charles Warren
Underground Jerusalem
R. Bentley & Son, 1876

Vincent Brian Wigglesworth
The Principles of Insect Physiology
Methuen, 1939

Leonard William Wing
Natural History of Birds
New York: Ronald Press Co., 1956

I. M. Wise
The World of My Books
Cincinnati, OH: American Jewish Archives, 1954

3

NOVELS

?
Sir Walter Newman Flower
Cassell, 1925

!!!
George Hughes Hepworth
New York: Harper & Bros., 1881
Hepworth was the author of **Through Armenia on Horseback**
(Isbister and Co., 1898).

Hugging to Music; or, The Waltz to the Grave. A Sketch from Life
'An American Observer'
M. J. Darg, 1889
A moralistic tale featuring Joe Jungle, the Wayback Infidel.

'Victoria Lennox entered the conservatory on the arm of Deluth, as the latter exclaimed: "Deny it! Deny it if you can!" The dreamy, waltz-intoxicated Victoria was speechless. A grasp on the portière at her side relaxed and Jack Lennox fell senseless at the feet of his terrified wife ...

"Miss Rodney, will you honour me with the next waltz?"

"Well now," said Aunt Sophronie as she tipped back with indignation, "why don't you speak plain English and ask me to hug you?"

"...what would you call that if you had me in your arms 15 or 20 minutes without the music?"

"Oh, dreadful," exclaimed Deluth.'

The Missing Fanny. A Tale of the Divorce Court
Anon.
n.p., c.1880

The Joy of the Upright Man
'J. B.'
n.p., 1619

When Woman Reigns
August Anson
Oxford: Pen-In-Hand Publishing Co.,
1938

Don't Point that Thing
at Me
After You with the Pistol
Something Nasty in the
Woodshed
Kyril Bonfiglioli
Black Spring Press, 1991

We All Killed Grandma
Fredric Brown
T. V. Boardman, 1954

'From the very topmost
drawer of Fredric Brown's
writing table.'

Riggermortis
Frank Bruno
Robert Hale, 1966

From the blurb: 'The sleepy-eyed albino drifter who rose to become
briefly known to contemporary fight fame as Tommy Riggermortis was
actually a chance Pugmalion [*sic*] created by the Bishop, to gratify a
long-nursed bizarre scheme of vengeance.'

Cockeye Kerrigan, *another novel by Frank Bruno, was described as*
containing 'Hard-knuckled pages blazing with biff and stingo . . .'

Riggermortis

FRANK BRUNO

What Will He Do With It?
Edward George Earle Lytton Bulwer-Lytton
Edinburgh: William Blackwood, 1859

Not Like Other Girls
Rosa Carey
Bentley, 1885

Tosser, Gunman
Frank Carr
Ward Lock & Co., 1939

> '"Gee! If it ain't Tosser Smith. What are you doin' in this neck of the country?"
> The cook stiffened as through his brain flashed the recollection of his recent attitude towards his visitor. His mouth became curiously dry. Tosser Smith, gunman, killer, outlaw. He'd heard tell that Tosser had killed more men than any other gunman known to the country.'

Pamela Pounce: A Tale of Tempestuous Petticoats
Agnes and Egerton Castle
Hodder & Stoughton, 1921

The Girl from the Big Horn Country
Mary Ellen Chase
George G. Harrap, 1937

Planet of the Knob Heads
Stanton A. Coblentz
Science Fiction, *Atlas Publishing, 1939*

> 'Jack and Marjorie are brought to the distant world of their captors. In far Andromeda, they struggle against "favors" of the knob-heads – but hope fades as they face the High Knobule!'
> 'In about a week I had recovered from most of the effects of the knob operation.'

Every Inch a Soldier

M. J. Colquhoun (the pseudonym of
Mrs Courtenay Scott)
Chatto & Windus, 1888

The Toff Goes Gay

John Creasey
Evans Brothers, 1951

Bek's First Corner

J. M. Conklin
John E. Shaw, 1883
Subtitled: 'and how she turned it'.

The Garden of Ignorance. The Experiences of a Woman in a Garden

Marion Cran
Herbert Jenkins, 1913

Cran was also the author of:

The Garden of Experience
Herbert Jenkins, 1922

The Joy of the Ground
Herbert Jenkins, 1928

The Lusty Pal
Herbert Jenkins, 1930

The Story of my Ruin
Herbert Jenkins, 1924

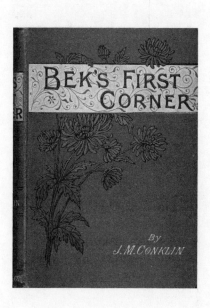

The Private Life of Helen of Troy
John Erskine
New York: Popular Library, 1948

'A gay, witty novel about a lovely woman to whom men first lost their hearts, then their heads, and finally their lives!'

The Fangs of Suet Pudding
Adams Farr
Gerald G. Swan, 1944

'In the heart of France, May 1940 . . . Loreley Vance is suddenly awakened from her sleep by the entry into her room of, so she thought, a burglar. It may be that because he happened to be English, handsome, young and appealing . . . she allowed him to hide under her bed, but whatever the reason it began the series of strange and startling events that brought her into the orbit of "Suet Pudding Face" Carl Vipoering, the master Nazi Spy, whose tentacles had spread over a small band of English folk who dared to oppose his machinations.

'Even the addition to their party of two fleeing Dictators fails to quench the courageous and ingenious zest of the little band. They care neither for the dignity of the Dictator, or the Teuton thoroughness of a Nazi. How, in spite of "Suet Pudding" Carl Vipoering's most vicious efforts, they smuggle themselves and their two highly-inflammable charges out of the country, and perhaps, alter the whole course of the war, makes a story which will hold your interest and has all the bubble and sparkle of its native champagne.'

Gay Cottage
Glance Gaylord (pseudonym of Ives Warren Bradley)
Boston, MA: American Tract Society, 1866

Man-Crazy Nurse
Peggy Graddis
Pyramid Books, 1967

What Farrar Saw
James Hanley
Nicholson & Watson, 1946

'No story by Mr Hanley is without its moral implications; here we have a glimpse of nightmare horror and chaos in a monstrous machine-ridden world. It starts simply enough as chaos does. A young couple set off for a holiday in Scotland. There is a road crash which causes a traffic block over half the country. Thousands of cars have to be abandoned. Their owners, suddenly condemned to a homeless, gypsy existence, lay siege to the neighbouring towns and villages. This is no book for the wishful thinker. It is a savage book and in its way a terrifying one, yet it has its lyrical passages of great beauty.'

Dildo Kay
Nelson Hayes
Boston, MA: Houghton Mifflin, 1940

The Shunned Vicar of the Gilliflowers
Frederick William von Herbert
Andrew Melrose, 1914

'The First Part setteth forth how the Vicar of the Gilliflowers quarrelled with the Judge of the Village and eke with the people thereof, and could by no manner of means make peace again . . .

How the grave of the wife of the Vicar was defiled by evil persons . . . How the Vicar implored the people to come to church and no one would . . .

The Second Part setteth forth how the Vicar struggled bravely albeit in vain . . . How evildoers poisoned the cat . . . How the Vicar prepared a feast, naming it with the name of Bazaar . . . the enemies of the Vicar prepared a feast more gorgeous than the feast of the Vicar . . . How the Vicar lost all his friends, and was an-hungered and in desperation . . .

The Third Part setteth forth how the Vicar, having accepted defeat . . . lived for five years in loneliness . . .

How the Vicar found a little boy and tended him. How the little boy died and was buried . . .'

E
Julian Hinckley
John Long, 1917

'The complete and somewhat mad history of the family of Montague Vincent, Esq., Gent.'

Mated with a Clown
Lady Constance Howard
F. V. White, 1884

Appleby on Ararat
Michael Innes
Victor Gollancz, 1941
'Makes rival detective stories look like allotments' *Times Literary Supplement*

The Bride Wore Weeds
Hank Janson (pseudonym of Stephen Daniel Frances)
Gaywood Press, 1950
'Best of Tough Gangster Authors'.
Janson was also the author of Lady Mind That Corpse, Sweetie Hold Me Tight, Slay Ride for Cutie *and* Honey Take My Gun.

The Strangest Grand National
Frank Johnston
John Long, 1947

'This is the amazing story of the adventures of four men who set out to win the Grand National by grafting kangaroo glands into a steeple-chaser, and at the same time amass a fortune from the bookmakers. Without doubt *The Strangest Grand National* is more exciting than Frank Johnston's *Million Dollar Gamble*, which Lord Rosebery in a letter to the author declared was so interesting and amusing.'

They Die With Their Boots Clean
Gerald Kersh
Heinemann, 1942

> 'A man gets knifed. A throat gets slit. A bomb goes off . . . As Sergeant Nelson talks his right eye blinks in the smoke of his cigarette. Pensively pursing his lips, he takes his left eye out, polishes it against the bosom of his battle-blouse, and puts it back again. "Is it in straight, Dusty?"'

Fine Weather Dick
Caroline W. Leakey
The Religious Tract Society, 1882

The Ups and Downs of Lady Di
Annie M. Lyster
National Society's Depository, 1907

Lost on Brown Willy
Arthur Noel Malan
Frederick Warne, 1890
In a series of 'Attractive and Interesting Stories'.

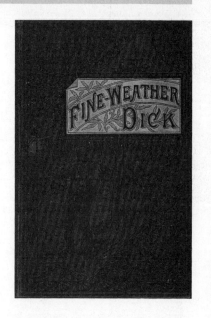

Gay Agony
Harold Alfred Manhood
Cape, 1930
Manhood was also the author of
Nightseed, Fierce and Gentle, Crack of Whip, Maiden's Fury *and* **Lunatic Broth.**

How Nell Scored
Bessie Marchant (afterwards Comfort)
Thomas Nelson & Sons, 1929, 2nd edition, 1952

How Nell Scored

BESSIE MARCHANT

Lesbia's Little Blunder
Bessie Marchant (afterwards Comfort)
Frederick Warne, 1934

The Adventures of Conrad the Cock
Princess Nusrat (pseudonym of Elizabeth Marc)
Hutchinson & Co., 1922

Mated from the Morgue
John Augustus O'Shea
Spencer Blackett, 1889

The Romance of a Dull Life
Mrs A. J. Penny
Longman, Green, 1861

Rabbits. A novel of realism
Alex J. Philip
Gravesend: Mariner Press, 1946

'The Book is a phantasy of what a world of men and women would be like if a superior people descended on them as "sportsmen" descend on the rabbits in a warren. It is a highly entertaining object lesson rather than a novel with a purpose. Now and then, perhaps, the reader may get that "cold feeling" down the spine.'

'This is a novel with a purpose, the purpose being more important than the romantic element.'

The Mariner Press specialises in books by librarians including: The Adventures of Bunny Manx, The Four Jays, The Naughty Coyote, Rabbit Warren *and* Six Wee Pigs.

Kinky Finds the Clue

Michael Poole (pseudonym of
Reginald Heber Poole)
George Newnes, 1948

> 'Ken "Kinky" Kinsmith soon found
> that there was more to the affair
> than a missing schoolboy . . .'

The Day Amanda Came

C. T. Reeves
Eastbourne: Victory Press, 1971

Queer Doings at Quantham

Wilfrid Robertson
Frederick Warne, 1956

Tombstones Are Free to Quitters

Ben Sarto
Modern Fiction Ltd, 1949

> '"I guess that guy got too much
> neck," Bigfella said. "But I reckon
> I twist it okay."'

The Negro's Ring

Philip Scott
Hutchinson, 1954

> 'The negro fell silent then . . .
>   "Do you come from the South?"
>   "From Kentucky and the Old
> Plantation."
>   "Gosh," said Jeremy. "It must
> have been pretty ghastly there in
> the slave days, wasn't it?"'

Misogyny Over the Week-end
Ronald McNair Scott
Macmillan, 1931

'This novel . . . pictures the pilgrimage of youth in search of love and beauty. It displays an unusual combination of wit and poetry, disillusionment and realism, audacity and taste.'

Boss of Bender County
Bart Segundo (pseudonym of Donald Sydney Rowland)
Robert Hale, 1964

Every Inch a Sailor
William Gordon Stables
Nelson, 1897

The Sauciest Boy in the Service: A Story of Pluck and Perseverance
William Gordon Stables
Ward, Lock & Co., 1905

Roger the Scout
Herbert Strang and George Lawrence
Henry Frowde, Hodder & Stoughton, 1910

Fellow Fags
Ethel Talbot
Sheldon Press, 1925

The Bungalow of Dead Birds
George Varney
Thomas Nelson, 1929

ROGER the SCOUT

HERBERT STRANG
AND
GEORGE LAWRENCE

Christie's Old Organ

Mrs O. F. (Amy Catherine) Walton
Religious Tract Society, 1882

'. . . when he had eaten his cake, and had taken some tea which he had warmed over again, old Treffy felt rather better, and he turned as usual to his old organ to cheer his fainting spirits. For old Treffy knew nothing of a better Comforter . . .

"Shall I take the organ out?"

Old Treffy did not answer; a great struggle was going on in his mind. Could he let any one but himself touch his dear old organ? It would be hard to see it go out, and have to stay behind – very hard indeed.'

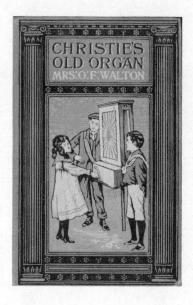

My Poor Dick

John Strange Winter (pseudonym of Henrietta Eliza Vaughan Stannard)
F. V. White, 1888

4

LANGUAGE

The Case for Latin in Bombay
A. Ailinger
Bombay: The Times *Press, 1940*

Rubbing Along in Burmese
Anon.
Simla: Directorate of Welfare and Education, Adjutant General's Branch GHQ, 1944

La Langue Bleue
Léon Bolak
Paris: Éditions de la Langue Bleue, Bolak Ditort, 1902

The New Guide of the Conversation in Portuguese and English in Two Parts
Pedro Carolino
Peking 'And to the house of all the booksellers of Paris', 1869, 2nd edition

Preface to the 2nd edition

'A choice of *familiar dialogues*, clean of gallicisms, and despoiled phrases, it was missing yet to studious portuguese and brazillian Youth; and also to persons of other nations, that wish to know the portuguese language. We sought all we may do, to correct that want, composing and divising the present little work in two parts. The first includes a greatest vocabulary proper names by alphabetical order; and the second forty three *Dialogues* adapted to the usual precisions of the life. For that reason we did put, with a scrupulous exactness, a great variety own expressions to english and portuguese idioms; without to attach us selves (as make some others) almost at a literal translation; translation what only will be for to accustom the portuguese pupils, or-foreign, to speak very bad any of the mentioned idioms.

We were increasing this second edition with a phraseology, in the first part, and some familiar letters, anecdotes, idiotisms, proverbs, and to second a coin's index.

The *Works* which we were confering for this labour, fond use us for nothing; but those what were publishing to Portugal, or out, they were almost all composed for some foreign, or for some national little aquainted in the spirit of both languages. It was resulting from that corelessness to rest these *Works* fill of imperfections, and anomalies of style; in spite of the infinite typographical faults which some times, invert the sense of the periods. It increase not to contain any of those *Works* the figured pronunciation of the english words, nor the prosodical accent in the portuguese: indispensable object whom wish to speak the english and portuguese languages correctly.

We expect then, who the little book (for the care what we wrote him, and for her typographical correction) that may be worth the acceptation of the studious persons, and especialy of the Youth, at which we dedicate him particularly.'

Familiar Phrases

Let us go on ours feet.

At what o'clock is to get up?

At which is this hat?

Have him some children?

At what o'clock dine him?

That is also.

Dress your hairs.

These apricots and these peaches make me and to come water in mouth.

How does you do to?

This ink is white.

This room is filled of bugs.

This girl have a beauty edge.

Tell that do you will do.

Undress you to.

Exculpate me by your brother's.

She do not that to talk and to cackle.

Are you in the bed yet?

It is she dressed?

She make the prude.

There is it two years what my father is dead.

It not rains.

It thinders.

It lightens.

He laughs at my nose, he jest by me.

He has scratch the face with hers nails.

He refuse to marry one's self.

He is valuable his weight's gold.

He caresses all women.

I have hungry.

I have trinked too much.

I have pains on to concieve me.

I have mind to vomit.

I am catched cold in the brain.

I shall not tell you than two woods.

Dress my horse.

What time from the month you are to-day?

Every man is exposed to make himself.

Your parents does exist yet?

Never I have you rumbled.

Dialogue 35 – With a Bookseller

What is there in new's litterature?

Little or almost nothing, it not appears any thing of note.

And yet one imprint many deal.

That is true; but what it is imprinted. Some news papers, pamphlets, and others ephemeral pieces; here is.

But why, you and another book seller, you does not to imprint some good works?

There is a reason for that, it is that you cannot to sell its. The actual-liking of the public is depraved they does not read who for to amuse one's self ant but to instruct one's.

But the letter's men who cultivate the arts and the sciences they can't to pass without the books.

A little learneds are happies enough for to may to satisfy their fancies on the literature.

What is the price of this fine Shakspeare edition?

A hundred and fifty franks.

Have you not found the Buffon who I had call for?

I have only been able to procure the octo-decimo edition, which is embellished with plates beautifully coloured.

When do you think you will publish your new catalogue?

It will appear without fait towards the end of the month.

Remember that I want a copy.

You shall be supplied one of the first.

Familiar Letters

Madam of Sevigné at their daughter
I write you every day: it is a jay which give me most favourable at all who beg me some letters. They will to have them for to appear before you, and me I don't ask better. That shall be given by M. D***. I don't know as he is called; but at last it is a honest man, what seems me to have spirit, and that me have seen here together.

Idiotisms and Proverbs

Few, few the bird make her nest.

The walls have hearsay.

He has a part in the coke.

He has the throat paved.

He is not valuable to breat that he eat.

Its are some blu stories.

Nothing some money, nothing of Swiss.

He steep as a marmot.

He has a good beak.

To build castles in Espagnish.

To eat of the cow mad.

That which feel one's snotly blow one's nose.

To buy a cat in pocket.

The stone as roll not heap up not foam.

The mountain in work put out a mouse.

Belly famished has no ears.

Take the moon with the teeth.

After the paunch comes the dance.

To craunch the marmoset.

AN IRISHMAN'S DIFFICULTIES
WITH THE DUTCH LANGUAGE

BY

EIGHTH EDITION   CUEY-NA-GAEL

J. M. BREDÉE'S UITGEVERS MIJ.- ROTTERDAM

An Irishman's Difficulties with the Dutch Language

'Cuey-na-Gael' (pseudonym of the Rev. Dr John Irwin Brown)
Rotterdam: J. M. Bredee, 1908
Such was the success (it went through eight editions between 1908 and 1928) of this genial guide that a further volume was published, entitled
O'Neill's Further Adventures in Holland.

What to Say When You Talk to Yourself

Shad Helmstetter
Scottsdale, AZ: Grindle Press, 1982

Laundry Lists with Detachable Counter-checks in French, Spanish, Portuguese, German, Italian, including Vocabularies and Necessary Phrases with Phonetic Spelling

W. J. Hernan
Eyre & Spottiswoode, 1909

Correctly English in Hundred Days

Min Hou and Lin Yutong (eds.)
Shanghai: English Translation Advancement Society, Correctly English Society, 1934

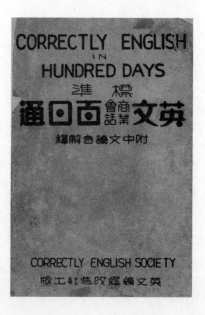

'This book is prepared for the Chinese young man who wishes to served for the foreign firms. It divided nealy hundred and ninety pages. It contains full of ordinary speak and write language. This book is clearly, easily, to the Chinese young man or scholar. If it is quite understood, that will be satisfaction.'

The Memoir of the Late Honorable Justice Onoocool Chunder Mookerjee
Mohindronauth Mookerjee
Serampore, 1873; 2nd edition,
Calcutta: Thacker, Spink, 1876

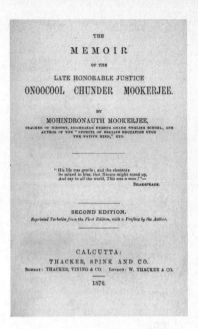

'The first edition of this humble and unassuming treatise was assailed on all sides by Nature and European Papers when it was ushered before the public, so much so that I lost all hopes of seeing a second edition of it . . . I do candidly admit, that I unfortunately threw myself open to some of the criticisms which I justly merited . . .'

Correct Mispronunciations of Some South Carolina Names
Claude and Irene Neuffer
Columbia, SC: University of South Carolina Press, 1984

How to Write While You Sleep
Elizabeth Irvin Ross
Cincinnati, OH: Writer's Digest Books, 1985

A French Letter Writing Guide
D. Sephton
Wicklewood: Primrose, 1980

What to Talk About
Imogene B. Wolcott
New York: G. P. Putnam's Sons, 1923

5
NATURE: FAUNA

Guide to the Deposit of Micro-Organisms Under the Budapest Treaty
Anon.
World Intellectual Property Organization, 2001

The Second-hand Parrot: A Complete Pet Owner's Manual
Mattie Sue Athan and Dianalee Deter
Hauppauge, NY: Barron's, 2002

Harnessing the Earthworm
Thomas J. Barrett
Faber & Faber, 1949

Fishes I Have Known
Arthur Henry Beavan
T. Fisher Unwin, 1905
Beavan was also the author of Birds I Have Known *and* Marlborough House and Its Occupants.

Homing Budgerigars
The Duke of Bedford
Cage Birds, 1953

Sex and Death in Protozoa: History of an Obsession
Graham Bell
New Rochelle, NY: Cambridge University Press, 1989

Where's Arthur's Gerbil?

Marc Tolon Brown
New York: Random House, 1997

Pigs I Have Known

Sacha Carnegie (pseudonym of Raymond Alexander Carnegie)
Peter Davies, 1958

The Flat-Footed Flies of Europe

Peter J. Chandler
Leiden: Brill, 2000

Charlie and his Dog Shag

'Charlie'
W. Kent & Co., 1877

Carnivorous Butterflies

Austin Hobart Clark
Washington, DC: United States Government Printing Office, 1926

Swine Judging for Beginners

Joel Simmonds Coffey
Columbus, OH: Ohio State University, 1915

The Rubaiyat of a Scotch Terrier

Sewell Collins
Grant Richards, 1926

Ducks & How to Make Them Pay

William Cook
St Mary Cray & London, 1890

277 Secrets Your Snake and Lizard Wants [sic] You to Know: Unusual and Useful Information for Snake Owners and Snake Lovers

Paulette Cooper
Berkeley, CA: Ten Speed Press, 1999

To Know a Fly
Vincent Gaston Dethier
San Francisco, CA: Holden-Day, 1962

The Romance of the Beaver
Arthur Radclyffe Dugmore
Heinemann, 1914

Collectanea
Sir Peter Eade
Jarrold & Sons, 1908

'I have in my garden two common land tortoises (*Testudo Graeca*). They are known by the names of the *old gentleman* and the *young gentleman*. They have lived on my premises and thriven for three or four years. They have become almost pets.'

Eade's Temperance and Tortoises *includes a detailed record of the behaviour of his two pets, including a table of their weights year by year, between 1886 and 1892, during which time both tortoises increased their weight by exactly 9 1/2 ounces.*

Canadian National Egg Laying Contests
F. C. Elford and A. G. Taylor
Ottawa: Department of Agriculture, 1924

Assessments and Decisions: A Study of Information Gathering by Hermit Crabs
Robert W. Elwood and S. J. Neil
Chapman & Hall, 1992

The Supernatural History of Worms
Marion C. Fox
Friends' Book Centre, 2nd edition, 1931

Rats for Those Who Care
Susan Fox
Neptune City, NJ: TFH Publications, 1995

Fish Who Answer the Telephone ➤
Yury Petrovich Frolov
Kegan Paul, Trench, Trübner, 1937

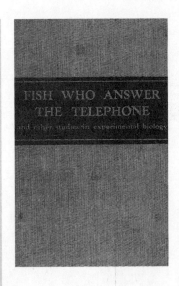

'Frolov is a Russian scientist of international repute . . . and has worked with some of the most famous men of our time, including Pavlov, the great physiologist.'

His experiment to prove that fishes can hear was conducted by making a telephone call.

'At first the telephone call was low toned, and the fish did not answer. But it was affected by the electrical shock. After we had repeated the experiment 40 times, we observed that the fish moved several seconds before the current was applied. It had come to know what the sound of the telephone meant, that it heralded the unpleasantness of the electric shock. The fish had heard the call from the submerged telephone. That was a real triumph.'

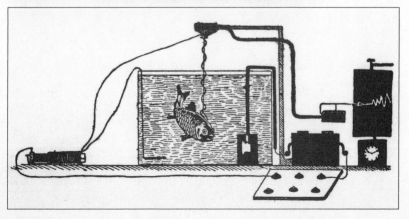

Show Biz Tricks for Cats: 30 Fun and Easy Tricks You Can Teach Your Cat

Anne Gordon and Steve Duno
Holbrook, MA: Adams Media, 1996

Understand Your Tortoise

K. A. Gray
Exmouth: The Author, c.1980

Enjoy Your Turtle

Richard Haas
The Pet Library, n.d.

'Bring a turtle into your house. There may not be much you can teach him, but perhaps there are lessons he can teach you.'

Ferret Facts and Fancies

A. R. Harding
Columbus, OH: The Author, 1915

Optical Chick Sexing

James E. Hartley and Ronald Hook
Nelson: Expert Chick Sexers, c.1954

Hippy. In Memoriam. The Story of a Dog

Sir Nevile Meyrick Henderson
Hodder & Stoughton, 1942

Sir Nevile Henderson was British Ambassador to the German Third Reich and published a biography of his dachsbracke, illustrated with several photographs, including 'Sir Nevile Henderson with Hippy at a Royal Shoot at the summer residence of the late King Alexander of Yugoslavia'.

The Goldfish of China in the 18th Century

George John Frangopulo Hervey
China Society, 1950

Anaesthesia and Narcosis of Animals and Birds

Sir Frederick Thomas George Hobday
Baillière & Co., 1915

Hobday was also the author of:
Castration
Edinburgh: W. and A. K. Johnston, 2nd edition, 1914

Did a Hen or an Egg Exist First? or, my Talks with a Sceptic

Jacob Horner
Religious Tract Society, c.1890

An Annotated Bibliography on Sea-Cucumbers

D. B. James
Cochin, India: Central Marine Fisheries Research Institute, 1994

A Letter to the Man Who Killed My Dog

Richard Joseph
New York: Frederick Fell, 1956

Flattened Fauna: A Field Guide to Common Animals of Roads, Streets, and Highways

Roger M. Knutson
Berkeley, CA: Ten Speed Press, 1987

'Why an animal is on the road and what it was doing there a few hours earlier are recorded in its flat remains as surely as the history of a tree is recorded in its annual rings.'

Insect Musicians and Cricket Champions of China

Berthold Laufer
Chicago, IL: Field Museum of Natural History, 1927

Ostrich Egg-shell Cups of Mesopotamia and the Ostrich in Ancient and Modern Times
Berthold Laufer
Chicago, IL: Field Museum of Natural History, 1926

Crab, Shrimp and Lobster Lore
William Barry Lord
George Routledge & Sons, 1867

The Onion Maggot
Arthur L. Lovett
Corvallis, OR: Agricultural Experimental Station, 1923

Keeping a Horse Outdoors
Susan McBane
Newton Abbott: David & Charles, 2003

Who's Who in Boxers
Marion Frances Robinson Mangrum
College Station, TX: n.p., 1950

Favourite Flies and their Histories
Mary Orvis Marbury
Boston, MA: Charles T. Branford & Co., 1955

Full Revelations of a Professional Rat-catcher after 25 Years' Experience
Ike Matthews
Manchester: Friendly Societies' Printing Co., 1898

Fifty New Creative Poodle Grooming Styles
Faye Meadows
New York: Arco Publishing Co., 1981

The Home-Life and Economic Status of the Double-Crested Cormorant
Howard Lewis Mendall
Orono, ME: University Press, 1936

Memorandum on the Size, Sex and Condition of Lobsters
Ministry of Agriculture and Fisheries
HMSO, 1912

Gay Neck: The Story of a Pigeon
Dhan Gopal Mukerji (Mukhopadhyaya Dhana-Gopala)
Illustrated by Boris Artzybasheff
J. M. Dent, 1928

Without Regret: A Handbook for Owners of Canine Amputees
Susan Neal
Sun City, AZ: Doral Publishing, 2002

The Joy of Chickens
Dennis Nolan
Englewood Cliffs, NJ: Prentice-Hall, 1981

Proceedings of the Second International Workshop on Nude Mice
T. Nomura, N. Ohsawa, N. Tamaoki and K. Fujiwara (eds.)
Tokyo: University of Tokyo Press, 1978

Enjoy Your Skunks
Helen Perley
New York: The Pet Library, 1967

British Tits
Christopher Perrins
Collins, 1979

Life and Love in the Aquarium
C. H. Peters
New York: Empire Tropical Fish Import Co., 1934

Fighting the Fly Peril

C. F. Plowman, et al.
T. Fisher Unwin, 1915

A Nostalgia for Camels

Christopher Rand
Boston, MA: Atlantic Monthly Press and Little, Brown and Co., 1957

Birds of the Mid-Atlantic, and Where to Find Them

John H. Rappole
Baltimore, MD: John Hopkins University Press, 2002

What's Wrong with My Snake?

John & Roxanne Rossi
Mission Viejo, CA: The Herpetocultural Library, 1996
The book contains photographs of: 'Chondropython necroscopy
showing severe pneumonia with chunks of pus', *the fractured neck of
a snake that got its head stuck under a door, one that managed to
swallow its own jaw and a boa fatally injured by a ferret.*

What's Wrong with My Iguana?

John Rossi
Mission Viejo, CA, Advanced Vivarium Systems Inc. 1999

Illustrated Catalogue of the Rothschild Collection of Fleas (Siphonaptera) in the British Museum (Natural History)

Miriam Rothschild, et al.
*Oxford: Oxford University Press/British Museum (Natural History), 7 vols.,
1953–87*

What is a Cow?: And Other Questions That Might Occur to You When Walking the Thames Path

David Sadtler
Cheltenham: Devon Publishing, 2000

Enjoy Your Chameleon

Earl Schneider
Harrison, NJ: The Pet Library, n.d.

FIGHTING
THE
FLY PERIL

With the Compliments of
BORAX CONSOLIDATED LTD

Enjoy Your Gerbils
Earl Schneider
Harrison, NJ: The Pet Library, 1979

The Art of Faking Exhibition Poultry
George Ryley Scott
T. Werner Laurie, 1934
The author treads an indistinct line between condemning this widespread and despicable practice, and telling the reader exactly how to do it.

Scott also wrote books on: nudism, birth control, flogging, capital punishment, torture, prostitution, obscene libel, sex guides, venereal disease, cockfighting, rejuvenation and phallic worship.

Thought Transference (or What?) in Birds
Edmund Selous
Constable, 1931; part 2, 1933

Elements of the Organic Enamel of the Hedgehog
John Silness
Bergen: Universitetsforlaget, 1967

The Guide to Owning a Quaker Parrot
Gayle Soucek
Neptune City, NJ: TFH, 2002

Monograph of the Horny Sponges
R. Von Lendenfeld
Royal Society of London, 1889

The Cult of the Budgerigar
William Erroll Glanville Watmough
Cage Birds, 1935

The Longevity of Starved Cockroaches

Edwin R. Willis and Norman Lewis

Reprinted from The Journal of Economic Entomology, *1957*

On Canine Madness

William Youatt

The Veterinarian, 1830

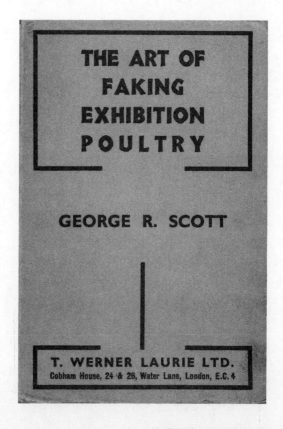

THE ART OF
FAKING
EXHIBITION
POULTRY

GEORGE R. SCOTT

T. WERNER LAURIE LTD.
Cobham House, 24 & 26, Water Lane, London, E.C. 4

6

NATURE: FLORA

Beyond Leaf Raking
Peter Benson and Eugene C. Roehlkepartain
Nashville, TN: Abingdon Press, 1994

**The Common Teasel as a
Carnivorous Plant**
Miller Christy
Journal of Botany, *1922*

Hairy Roots
Pauline M. Doran
Taylor & Francis, 1997

Gardening with Brains
Henry Theophilus Finck
New York: Harper & Brothers, 1922

**Nutmeg Cultivation and
its Sex-problem**
M. Flach
*Wageningen: H. Veenman & Zonen,
1966*

Gardening with Compost
F. C. King
Faber & Faber, 1944

*HOW TO ENJOY
YOUR WEEDS*

Audrey Wynne Hatfield

Gardening
with
Compost

F.C.KING

Introduction by
Sir *ALBERT HOWARD*

How to Enjoy Your Weeds
Audrey Wynne Hatfield
Frederick Muller, 1969

The Sleep of Plants
John Hill
Printed for R. Baldwin, 1757

Save Your Own Seed
Lawrence D. Hills
Braintree, Essex: Henry Doubleday, 1975

Studies on Bunt or Stinking Smut
Robert Whilmer Leukel
Washington, DC: United States Department of Agriculture, 1937

Proceedings of the Fifteenth International Seaweed Symposium
Sandra C. Lindstrom and David J. Chapman (eds.)
Dordrecht: Kluwer Academic Publishers, 1996

Of the Irritability of Vegetables
Robert Lyall
Nicholson's Journal xxiv, 1809

Thirty Years of Bananas
Alex Makula
Nairobi: Oxford University Press, 1993

The Giant Cabbage of the Channel Islands
Southcombe Parker and Gregory Stevens Cox
St Peter Port, Guernsey: Toucan Press, 1970

Carrots Love Tomatoes
Louise Riotte
Charlotte, VT: Garden Way, 1981

Trees to Know in Oregon
Charles R. Ross
*Corvallis, OR: Oregon State
University, 1978*

The History and Social
Influence of the Potato
Redcliffe Nathan Salaman
*Cambridge: Cambridge University
Press, 1970*

Heavy Metal Tolerance in
Plants
A. Jonathan Shaw
Boca Raton, FL: CRC Press, 1990

Gay Gardens from Seed
S. Baker Williams
W. H. & L. Collingridge, 1932

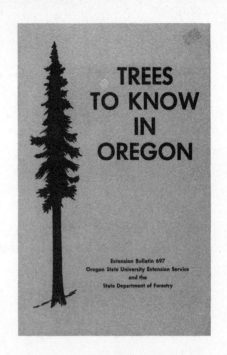

TREES
TO KNOW
IN
OREGON

Extension Bulletin 697
Oregon State University Extension Service
and the
State Department of Forestry

7

SCIENCE & SCIENTIFIC THEORIES

Petroleum in Leather

Anon.

Rochester, NY: Vacuum Oil Co., 1896

On curing leather. With an initial instruction to readers that all earlier editions should be thrown away.

'READ THIS FIRST. Begin again. Please destroy the book (*Better Stuffing-Grease*) which we sent you three years ago. This book is a careful effort to state in handy form for your guidance all we know of petroleum oils and greases in currying.

Our way in exploring a technical subject is to employ a chemist and a practical man; search continually by them; and, whenever we hit upon anything promising, go to the very highest learning there is for counsel upon it . . .

Estimate neither too high nor too low: this book is a safe start, if you estimate it as we desire, and some help on the way; it may or may not be sufficient. We shall try to do by letter what we fail to do by print. We are a learner as well as a teacher.

. . . fat ceases to keep the leather mellow and fresh, like new. But petroleum suffers no change . . Petroleum keeps out germs and stays, fat invites germs in and goes.

This is practical fact with some mixture of theory . . . A theory is a consistent system of statements concerning some subject, believed by learned men; of which system some parts are known to be true and the rest are believed; the whole explaining the recognized facts of the subject. It is not mere guessing even of learned men; it is partly fact, and the rest is supposed to be fact; and the learned are watching for evidence for and against it . . .

Practical men, advised by the learned, accept the whole germ theory almost as fact; but are always looking for evidence for and against the unproved parts of it. You had better accept it; at the same time, we have no right to assert the whole of it.'

There are many reasons to prefer petroleum to fat, for instance: 'Petrol stuffing contains no filth, unless you add filth to our grease. (The cheapest raw material of the "currier's grease" manufacturer is sewer grease. When sewage stands undisturbed for a little time, grease rises to the top. This grease is taken off and "refined". We have heard that butter is got from Thames mud; perhaps in the same way as currier's grease is got from sewage . . .'

But even petrol may not be the answer: 'CAUTION ABOUT PETROLEUM. There is a great variety of petroleum products. Some are so clearly of no use in leather that no one will ever try them; some seem promising but are of no value and are actually injurious; some are known to be useful, but the extent of their usefulness is not known; and some perhaps are pretty well known already . . .'

Confidence in the product is not unbounded: '. . . it is new, you are not accustomed to it; there are problems connected with it not yet solved by anybody. Every improvement meets these obstacles. (The time to learn new ways is when they are new.)'

The Coming Disaster Worse Than the H-bomb, Astronomically, Geologically and Scientifically Proven. The Coal Beds, Ice Ages, Tides, and Coming Soon, a Great Wave and Flood Caused by a Shift of the Axis of the Earth From the Gyroscopic Action of Our Solar System. Why Our Solar System Works.

Adam D. Barber

Washington, DC: Barber Scientific Foundation, 1954

Barber's theory is that the Earth shifts on its axis every 9,000 years, taking a mere ninety minutes to do so. The last occasion resulted in Noah's Flood; the next is imminent.

The Biochemist's Songbook

Harold Baum

Oxford: Pergamon Press 1982

'At last the ultimate best seller, sing-along-a-syllabus. These two sensational new packages take biology into a dimension never thought possible. Subjects such as excretion, reproduction, genetics, and evolution have been set to music by the world's leading exponent of the biological ballad, Professor Harold Baum and original music written by Peter Shade. Each package contains a book plus an audio cassette with the songs sung by a new group, *The Metabolites*.'

Twenty Beautiful Years of Bottom Physics

R. A. Burnstein, D. M. Kaplan and H. A. Rubin (eds.)

Berlin: Springer-Verlag, 1998

Water, Not Convex: The Earth Not a Globe!

William Carpenter

The Author, 1871

Carpenter was a British follower of "Parallax" (see page 82) and later emigrated to America to promote his Flat Earth Theory; there he wrote:
One Hundred Proofs that the Earth is Not a Globe
Baltimore, MD: The Author, 1885

Holes
Roberto Casati and Achille C. Varzi
MIT, 1994

Romping Through Physics
Otto Willi Gail
G. Routledge & Sons, 1933

On the Kyungrak System
Kim Bong Han
Pyonyang, D.P.R.K.: Foreign Languages Publishing House, 1964

'. . . Professor Kim Bong Han and his associates discovered the substance of Kyungrak, a new anatomico-histological system in the living body . . . entirely different either from the nervous system or blood and lymphatic vessels. . . Their research work [has] made further progress, blazing the trail along an untrodden path to divulge the secrets of the organism . . .'

The professor modestly named the newly discovered structures as Bonghan ducts (carrying Bonghan Liquor) and Bonghan corpuscles. Unfortunately, despite the 'deep concern' of Comrade Kim Il Sung, no other scientists followed the untrodden path as Kim Bong Han's discoveries were found to be entirely imaginary.

What's Wanted. A List of 895 Needed Inventions
Institute of Patentees
Institute of Patentees, 3rd edition, 1933

A useful source of ideas for the budding inventor, including:
- Lipstick-proof linen
- A bullet-proof stroboscope
- An automatic refrigerator for under £3.10s.0d.
- A machine for the dining table to pick winkles from their shells
- Improvements in deckchairs whereby the user can sit sideways
- A slot-machine for use at post offices to give two halfpennies for a penny
- A domestic machine for use in private houses for getting rid of books by pulping

Ultracool Dwarfs
H. R. A. Jones and I. A. Steele (eds.)
Berlin: Springer Verlag, 2001

How to Draw a Straight Line
Sir Alfred Bray Kempe
Macmillan, 1877

'The Unexplored Fields are still vast.'

Light and Truth. Martin's invention for destroying all foul air and fire damps in coal pits, and making the foulest pits as pure as the surface of this earth, etc. [W. (*sic.*) Martin proving the Scriptures to be right which learned men are mystifying, and proving the orang-outang, or monkey, the most unlikely thing under the sun to be the serpent that beguiled our first parents.]
Jonathan Martin
Newcastle on Tyne: Pattison & Ross, 1838

Jonathan Martin (1782–1838), the brother of John Martin, the painter of apocalyptic scenes, was found guilty of setting fire to York Minster in 1829.

The Impact of Global Warming on Texas
Gerald R. North, Jurgen Schmandt, and Judith Clarkson
Austin, TX: University of Texas Press, 1995

Wigglers, Undulators and Their Applications
Hideo Onuki & Pascal Elleaume (eds.)
Taylor & Francis, 2002

Zetetic Astronomy
'Parallax' (pseudonym of Samuel Birley Rowbotham)
Birmingham: W. Cornish, 1849

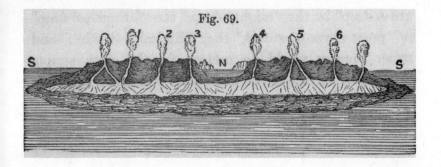

Fig. 69.

In a series of experiments conducted along the 'Bedford Level' in Cambridgeshire in 1838, 'Parallax' attempted to demonstrate that he could see distant objects sited on the canal and that cannon balls fired vertically fell straight down, thus proving that the Earth is flat and non-rotating. His findings were published in this remarkable work, the title of which derives from the Greek, meaning 'I discover for myself'. He had many zetetic followers, including William Carpenter (see page 80), Lady Elizabeth Anne Mould Blount, John Hampden, William Edgell (see page 87) and others who wrote books along similar lines, starting a 'Flat Earth' cult that continues to this day.

The Life-Romance of an Algebraist

George Winslow Pierce
Boston, MA: J.G. Cupples, 1891

The text is set vertically to the page; Harvard reminiscences of a mathematician poised between genius and madness:

> 'Full of power, and suspecting no weakness, I bent myself, after every snap, without a word, to the task before me; but the last snap snapped something in my head, behind, and a trembling thrill spread slowly over the cerebellum.'

Science of Nature-History. A line of study for assigning places to all events in creation in order of time, showing their genesis, which may define themselves

Nasarvanji Jivanji Readymoney
Bombay: The Times of India *Office, 1907*

'Nature-history means nature's knowledge, to know it by corresponding the order of ideas to the order of nature in time, that is the order of events in time. The Science of Nature-History is to discover the past by nature-history method and to record the past in such a manner as to investigate it and act upon it. Thus nature-history is the practical study of nature.'

As a 'specimen' Mr Readymoney cites H.M. King-Emperor Edward VII: '. . . military, priestly and civil Special actions of the King-Emperor have devolved upon him, that is, all his special actions with his own and foreign ministers, Emperors and subjects, meeting with Emperors, and saving Empire and enlarging or bringing prosperity to his subjects. Thus a nature-historian, without falling into the errors by religious or socialistic political bias or ignorance, will record events why it was natural that all those events should have taken place to bring into existence such a Monarch and the Empire . . .'

The certainty with which the author defines the natural order of things is undermined by five errata slips and four inserted pages. One of the errata suggests that the title itself is in error – probably unique in the History and Nature-History of publishing:

SCIENCE OF NATURE-HISTORY.

A line of study for assigning places to all events in creation in order of time, showing their genesis, which may define themselves

NOTE.

This work is entitled "Science of Nature-History," which is Science of History. For History and Nature-History are synonymous in a broad sense. The general public understand "Science of Nature-History" to be natural history. Therefore it could be better named "Science of History or Science of Nature-History." Wherever Nature-History is referred to in the text, it may be read as History. The meaning thereby does not change.

Helium in Canada from 1926 to 1931

P. V. Rosewarne
Ottawa: F. A. Acland, 1931

The Romance of Holes in Bread. A Plea for the Recognition of the Scientific Laboratory as the Testing Place for Truth

I. K. Russell
Easton, PA: The Chemical Publishing Co., 1924

A New General Theory of the Teeth of Wheels

Edward Sang
A&C Black, 1852
Sang was Professor of Mechanical Philosophy in the Imperial School, Muhendis-Hana Berrii, Constantinople.

Chemistrianity. (Popular Knowledge of Chemistry) A Poem; Also an Oratorical Verse on each known Chemical Element in the Universe, Giving Description, Properties, Sources, Preparation and Chief Uses

John Carrington Sellars
Birkenhead: The Author, c.1873

Seven Years of 'Manifold': 1968–1980

Ian Stewart and John Jaworski (eds.)
Nantwich: Shiva Publishing, c.1981

Answering mathematical problems (except how 1980 minus 1968 equals seven).

Scientific
Amusements

by Tom Tit

Scientific Amusements
Tom Tit (pseudonym of Arthur Good)
Translated from the French by Cargill Gilston Knott
T. Nelson & Sons, 1918

Improvement of the Steady Floating Random Walk Monte Carlo Method Near Straight Line and Circular Boundaries, with Application to Groundwater Flow
James Harold Turner
Manhattan, KA: Kansas Water Resources Research Institute, 1977

Does the Earth Rotate?
William Westfield (pseudonym of William Edgell)
Radstock: n.p., 1914

Westfield was also the author of:

Is the Earth a Fixture? Yes! And the Sun Travels
Bath: n.p., 1915

The Skeleton Edition of the Book of Comprehension No.1 The Preparation X.13: The Rose of Colour Reference for Technical, Kindergarten and Nature Teachers
Frederick J. Wilson
The Comprehensional Association, 1891

'Comprehension is to the better seeing what we look at; through our knowing the meanings to its Colour, its Form, and its Number, by which it is made visible to us.'

The author's statement of intention reports that he has 'published many expensive unappreciated pamphlets; which have been pronounced "incomprehensible".'

'The all-relation will be of the Forms and Numbers, and then of the 16 Professions proved to the Colours.'

8

WASTE PRODUCTS

An Essay Upon Wind; with Curious Anecdotes of Eminent Peteurs. Humbly Dedicated to the Lord Chancellor

Anon. (alleged to be Charles James Fox)

'Printed and sold by all the Booksellers in Town and Country', 1787

'I take it there are five or six different species of Farts, and which are perfectly distinct from each other, both in weight, and smell.

First, the sonorous, and full-toned Fart;

Second, the double Fart;

Third, the soft-fizzing Fart;

Fourth, the wet Fart . . .is very easily procured. Let any person fond of overeating, cram himself with pies, custards, whip-syllabub, prunes, &c. &c. and he will do his business with effectual dispatch, so as to need an immediate washing. Ladies produce this species of Fart better than gentlemen, so that it is adviseable to try this experiment upon a strong, healthy young lady of about eighteen, and who is apt to be hungry. . .

and Fifth, the sullen, wind bound Fart.'

Pooh! Pooh! A Poem By One of Job's Comforters

Anon.

n.p., 1839

Stray Leaves from Japanese Papers

Anon.

Bourne, Johnson & Latimer, c.1870

Also from the same publishers, but in paper covers rather than maroon cloth, **Nothing but Leaves.**

Comprises approximately 400 blank leaves of 'Japanese sanitary paper. Antiseptic. Hygienic. A Perfectly pure article for the toilet and lavatory, and a preventative for piles . . . as soft as silk and although it is very tough, will readily dissolve in water . . . confidently recommended as the best article ever produced for the particular purpose for which it is intended.'

Survey of toilet facilities for the public in chain stores, cooperative retail stores and department stores

Anon.
Stoke-on-Trent: British Ceramic Sanitaryware Manufacturers, 1965

Arresting Disclosures. A Report on the Strange Findings in Undergarments Washed with Soap and Water, and Popularly Supposed to be Clean, Fresh and Wholesome

John A. Bolton
Leicester: J. & J. H. Vice, 1924

The Urine Dance of the Zuni Indians of New Mexico

Captain John G. Bourke
Ann Arbor, MI: American Association for the Advancement of Science, 1885

The urine dance clearly made a lasting impression on Captain Bourke, for in 1891 he published a detailed treatise, Scatalogic Rites of all Nations *(Washington DC: W. H. Lowdermilk). It is subtitled,* A Dissertation upon the Employment of Excrementitious Remedial Agents in Religion, Therapeutics, Divination, Witchcraft, Love-Philters, &c. *The titlepage bears the legend,* 'NOT FOR GENERAL PERUSAL'.

A Sanitary Crusade through the East and Australia
Robert Boyle
Glasgow: Boyle, 1892

The Gas We Pass: The Story of Farts
Shinta Cho
Brooklyn, NY: Kane/Miller Book Publishers, 1994

The Muck Manual: A Practical Treatise on the Nature and Values of Manures
F. Falkner
John Murray, 1843

The Golden Fountain: Complete Guide to Urine Therapy
Coen van der Kroon
Banbury: Amethyst Books, 1996

Dirt: A Social History as Seen Through the Uses and Abuses of Dirt
Terence McLaughlin
New York: Stein & Day, 1971

How to Test Your Urine at Home
B. C. Meyrowitz
Girard, KS: Haldeman-Julius, c.1935

Sewage No Value. The Sewage Difficulty Exploded
Edward Monson
Spon, 1874

The Zen of Bowel Movements: A Spiritual Approach to Constipation
Kathy A. Price
Santa Barbara, CA: Rock House Pub., 1995

The Benefit of Farting Explain'd

Don Fartinhando Puffindorst
(pseudonym – probably
Jonathan Swift)
*Printed for A. Moore,
near St. Paul's, 1722*

*Thirteen London editions were
published in 1722; attribution is
traditionally to Jonathan Swift,
though he himself suggested 'one
Dobbs, a surgeon' as the author.*
It *was followed by:*
The benefit of farting farther
explained, vindicated, and
maintained, against those
blunderbusses who will not
allow it to be concordant to
the cannon law . . . By Fart-in-
Hand-o Puff-indorst, author of
the Fart à posteriori. Humbly
inscribed to Mine arse in a
bandbox. The second edition.
Printed for A. Moore,
and sold by the booksellers
[1722]

All About Mud

Oliver R. Selfridge
*Reading, MA: Addison-Wesley,
1978*

Dust and the Dustbin

Mrs Sheil
Home & Colonial School Society, n.d.

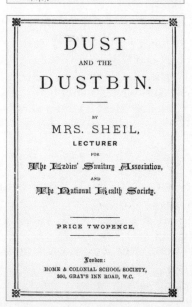

Anaerobic Sludge Digestion
Task Force on Anaerobic Sludge
Digestion
*Alexandria, VA: Water Pollution
Control Federation, 1987*

On the Composition of Farmyard Manure
Dr Augustus Voelcker
Printed by W. Clowes & Sons, 1856

Voelker later took another dip
into:

Liquid Manure
Printed by W. Clowes & Sons, 1859

England's True Wealth
William White
Groombridge & Sons, 1849

Subtitled England's True Wealth;
or Foecal Matters in Their
Application to Agriculture by
William White, Consulting
Chemist to the City of London
Portable Manure Company

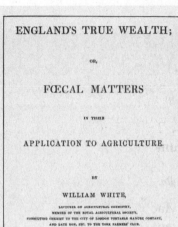

ENGLAND'S TRUE WEALTH;

OR,

FŒCAL MATTERS

IN THEIR

APPLICATION TO AGRICULTURE.

BY

WILLIAM WHITE,

LECTURER ON AGRICULTURAL CHEMISTRY,
MEMBER OF THE ROYAL AGRICULTURAL SOCIETY,
CONSULTING CHEMIST TO THE CITY OF LONDON PORTABLE MANURE COMPANY,
AND LATE HON. SEC. TO THE YORK FARMERS' CLUB.

LONDON:
GROOMBRIDGE AND SONS, 5, PATERNOSTER ROW.
1849.

9
HEALTH & MEDICINE

Exposure and Removal of the Brain
E. K. Adrian, Jr
Health Series Consortium, 1984

The Turkish Bath an Antidote for the Cravings of the Drunkard
J. A.
Dublin: R. D. Webb, 1859

A Madman's Musings . . . Written by A Patient During his Detention in a Private Madhouse
Anon.
A. E. Harvey, 1898

A Pictorial Book of Tongue Coating
Anon.
Kyoto: Yukonsha Publishing Co., 1981

From the publishers of A Complete Work of Acupuncture and Moxibustion *(25 vols.) comes a guide to the ancient Chinese method of diagnosis by examination of the tongue, which includes 257 coloured photographs of:*

11: Whitish tongue with a thin whitish moist slippery fur
25: Whitish tongue with reddened tip and thick yellowish white greasy fur
63: Pink tongue with red spots, purple speckles and thin whitish greasy fur
139: Dull red furless tongue with scanty slobber
196: Deep red tongue with a slippery moist 'mouldy sauce paste' fur
217: Bluish purple lean small tongue with a white rotten fur

Old Age: Its Cause and Prevention

Sanford Bennett
New York: Physical Culture Publishing Co., 1912

The electric face mask recommended 'is wonderfully effective and it certainly does whiten the skin and generally improve the complexion. If accurately fitted it will last a life time.' *Bennett is described as* 'the man who grew young at 70'.

The Romance of Proctology

Charles Elton Blanchard
Youngstown, OH: Medical Success Press, 1938

'The story of the history and development of this much neglected branch of surgery from its earliest times to the present day, including brief biographic sketches of those who were its pioneers.'

Humour Therapy in cancer, psychosomatic diseases, mental disorders, crime, interpersonal and sexual relationships.

Branko Bokun
Vita Books, 1986

'"Your theories make good sense – and the stories you use to illustrate the theories are delightful." Norman Cousins, who recovered from cancer, curing himself with humour therapy.'

Dentologia: A Poem on the Diseases of the Teeth and Their Proper Remedies

Solyman Brown (pseudonym of Eleazar Parmly)
New York: American Library of Dental Science, 1840

From a testimonial: 'On a subject so unpromising, I think all would agree with me in saying that the author has succeeded beyond all reasonable expectations.'

'One common destiny awaits our kind;–
'Tis this, that long before the infant mind
Attains maturity – and ere the sun
Has through the first septennial circle run,
The teeth, deciduous, totter and decay,
And prompt successors hurry them away . . .

Be watchful, ye – whose fond maternal arm
Would shield defenceless infancy from harm,
Mark well the hour when nature's rights demand
The skilful practice of the dentist's hand . . .

Derangement, pain and swift decay,
Obtain in man their desolating sway,
Corrupt his blood, infect his vital breath,
And urge him headlong to the shades of death.'

Colon Cleanse the Easy Way!

Vena Burnett and Jennifer Weiss
Orem, UT: Woodland Publishing, 1990

Burr Identification System of Breast Analysis

Timothy Burr
Trenton, NJ: Hercules Publishing Co., 1965

'. . . why and how women's breasts reveal their character . . . uniquely valuable dictionary-commentary on a thousand ways to describe women.' *Classification according to:* 'Bag shape; Content ratio; Bag angle; Nipple area and Diam/Ext ratio.'

Flushing and Morbid Blushing
Harry Campbell
H. K. Lewis, 1890

Fresh Air and How to Use It
Thomas Spees Carrington
New York: The National Association for the Study and Prevention of Tuberculosis, 1912

The Breath of Life; or, Mal-respiration, and Its Effects Upon the Enjoyment and Life of Man
George Catlin
New York: John Wiley, 1861

The book was later reissued as:

Shut your Mouth and Save your Life
N. Trübner & Co., 1869

Surplus Fat
William Francis Christie
Heinemann, 1927

Cluthe's Advice to the Ruptured ➤
Charles Cluthe
Bloomfield, NJ: Chas. Cluthe and Sons (of the Cluthe Rupture Institute), 71st edition, 1915

Testimonial from a satsified customer of Mr Cluthe: 'Quickly Cured, but Would Feel Lost Without It . . . Your truss cured me in about six months but as I feel lost without it, I am still wearing it.'

The Glands of Destiny
Ivo Geikie Cobb
Heinemann, 1927

Skin Diseases for Beginners
Richard Bertram Coles and Patrick David Clifford Kinmont
H. K. Lewis & Co., 1957

Trusses Like These Are A Crime

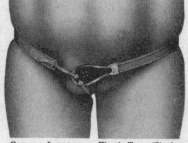

Common Leg strap or Elastic Truss (Single)

So-called "Appliances" are Usually Merely a Slight Adaptation of this Style of Truss—Merely the Most Worthless Kinds of Trusses Masquerading under Misleading Names.

How They Often Fool You By False Holding

A leg-strap or elastic truss usually has to be buckled up so tight you can scarcely stand to keep it on. The leg-straps are a constant annoyance. They pull the holding pad away from the real rupture opening and down on the pelvic bone, causing harmful pressure on the life-giving spermatic cord. The slightest strain — such as coughing or sneezing — is usually enough to force the rupture out. Such trusses often fool their wearers by false holding. Instead of sealing the real opening they often let the rupture come part way out and then squeeze it against the pelvic bone. That kind of holding is always dangerous.

The Cruel Spring Truss

It is impossible to keep the spring truss in position. Due to the force of the springs around the waist, the pads dig against the pelvic bone with terrible pressure, sapping the vitality. A previous chapter shows how most ruptures grow constantly worse when trusses like these are worn.

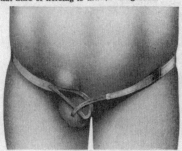

Why Spring Trusses Hurt So

Dotted lines in lower illustration show a Double Spring Truss coiled up before applied. Try to hold springs apart as when on the body as shown for half a minute. Then you will know what criminal pressure the spring truss gives.

On Consumption
George Thomas Congreve
The Author and Elliot Stock, 1887

'New and enlarged edition, with Appendix.'

Cancer: Is the Dog the Cause?
Samuel Walter Cort
John Bale, Sons & Danielsson, 1933

'I have an objection to being poisoned by a dog, to using dog-excreta dust as face-powder, as snuff, or as a condiment with my food.

The dog's street habits are repulsively dirty, and grossly indecent. It revels in filth, and will maul and eat putrefying flesh. It licks sores – and other things.

Its hair, teeth and saliva are poisonous.

. . . to keep a dog, to cuddle, fondle, stroke, kiss, or be kissed by a dog, is to invite disease and death.'

Psycho-Analysis for Normal People
Geraldine Coster
Oxford: Oxford University Press, 1926

Eleven Years a Drunkard, or, The Life of Thomas Doner, Having Lost Both Arms Through Intemperance, He Wrote this Book with His Teeth as a Warning to Others
Thomas Doner
Sycamore, IL: Arnold Bros., 1878

The Solar Plexus or Abdominal Brain

Theron Q. Dumont
*Chicago, IL: Advanced Thought
Publishing Co., 1920*

'The Fourth Brain of Man . . .
the seat of the emotional
nature of Man . . . the great
centre of the Sympathetic
Nervous System.'

The Encyclopedia of Medical Ignorance

Ronald Duncan and
M. Weston-Smith (eds.)
Oxford: Pergamon Press, 1984

How To Be Plump

Thomas Cation Duncan
Chicago, IL: Duncan Bros., 1878

A Treatise on the Stomach and Its Trials

James Crossley Eno
*Leeds: Newbery & Sons, 11th edition,
1881*

THE
STOMACH AND ITS TRIALS.

THE KEY-NOTE OF CREATION,
CHANGE !!!

"Oh! ever thus, from Childhood's hour, I've seen my
fondest hopes decay,
I never loved a tree, or flower, but 'twas the first to
fade away,
I never nursed a dear gazelle, to glad me with its soft
black eye,
But when it came to know me well and love me, it was
sure to die."—*Moore.*

'Yes; when I suffer from a brain overwrought –
Excited, feverish, worn, from laboured thought –
Harassed by anxious care, or sudden grief,
I run to Eno and obtain relief.'

New National Strength Through the Beauty of the Teeth

Henry C. Ferris
New York: The Author, 1919

The History of Cold Bathing
Sir John Floyer
S. Smith & B. Walford, 1706

'A Gentleman of the Temple, a hale man, of a strong athletick Habit . . . stayed in the cold bath of Mr Baynes at least 15 minutes . . . but it so chill'd him, that he had much ado to recover it, and was not well in some time . . .'

Secret of the Ring Muscles: Healing Yourself Through Sphincter Exercise
Paula Garbourg
Wayne, NJ: Avery Group, 1997

Sensors and Sensory Systems for an Electronic Nose
Julian W. Gardner and Philip N. Bartlett
Dordrecht: Kluwer Academic Publishers, 1992

The Inheritance of Hairy Ear Rims
Reginald Ruggles Gates and P. N. Bhaduri
Edinburgh: Mankind Quarterly, 1961

The Hive; or, Mental Gatherings. For the Benefit of the Idiot and His Institution
Eliza Grove
Earlswood: The Asylum for Idiots, 1857

A Study of Hospital Waiting Lists in Cardiff, 1953–1954
Fred Grundy
Cardiff: United Cardiff Hospitals, 1956

The Deadly Cigarette; or the perils of juvenile smoking
John Quincy Adams Henry
Richard J. James & British Lads' Anti-Smoking Union, 1906

Henry signs his frontispiece portrait 'Yours for the Boys' and dedicates the book to his son William Mellors Henry, 'who is pledged against smoking, drinking, gambling and swearing'.

Cycling as a Cause of Heart Disease
George Arieh Herschell
Baillière & Co., 1896

The Romance of the Spine
Irene F. Goodman
John Bale, Sons & Danielsson, 1935

'A brochure for those in quest of the Art of Life for cases of Postural Scoliosis.'

The Toothbrush: Its Use and Abuse
Isador Hirschfield
New York: Dental Items of Interest Publishing Co., 1939

On Leprosy and Fisheating: A Statement of Facts and Explanations
Sir Jonathan Hutchinson
Constable and Co., 1906

Inflammatory Bowel Diseases: A Personal View
H. D. Janowitz
Yearbook Medical Publishers, 1986

100,000,000 Guinea Pigs
Arthur Kallet and F. J. Schlink
New York: The Vanguard Press, 1933

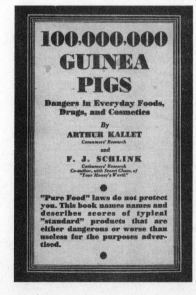

100,000,000 GUINEA PIGS

Dangers in Everyday Foods, Drugs, and Cosmetics

By
ARTHUR KALLET
Consumers' Research
and
F. J. SCHLINK
Consumers' Research
Co-author, with Stuart Chase, of
"Your Money's Worth"

"Pure Food" laws do not protect you. This book names names and describes scores of typical "standard" products that are either dangerous or worse than useless for the purposes advertised.

The Bicycle as a Factor in Genito-urinary Diseases, Prostatitis, Prostatorrhea or Prostatic Catarrh, (false spermatottmoea)

H. H. Kane
n.p., 1896; reprinted by Albert Saifer, 1983

Earology

J. K. Karmakar
Calcutta: Research Institute of Earology, 1981

Tells how to diagnose character and disease by study of the external ear.

The Itinerary of a Breakfast

John Harvey Kellogg
New York: Funk & Wagnalls Co., 1926

'A popular account of the travels of a breakfast through the food tube and of the ten gates aad [*sic*] several stations through which it passes, also of the obstacles which it sometimes meets.'

Hot Topics in Urology

Roger S. Kirby and Michael P. O'Leary
W.B. Saunders, 2003

The Art of Invigorating and Prolonging Life . . . To which is added The Pleasure of Making a Will

William Kitchiner
Hurst, Robinson, 1822

Dedicated to 'The Nervous and Bilious'.

My Water-Cure

Sebastian Kneipp
William Blackwood, 5th edition, n.d.

Let's Be Normal! The Psychologist Comes to His Senses

Fritz Kuenkel
New York: Ives Washburn, 1929

I Was a Mental Statistic

Edward Lane

New York: Carlton, 1963

Memoirs of an Amnesiac

Oscar Levant

Hollywood, CA: Samuel French, 1965

Coma Arousal

Edward B. Le Winn

New York: Doubleday, 1985

'No special equipment or expertise is necessary.'

The Fountain of Youth; or, Curing by Water. How You May Quickly Overcome Acute and Chronic Illness by the Use of the Biological Blood-Washing Bath

Dr Benedict Lust

Introduction by Bernarr Macfadden

New York: Macfadden Publications, 1923

Bernarr Macfadden refers in his introduction to Dr Lust's 'profound interest in Mr Christos Parasco's discovery' – *a discovery which* 'actually washes the poisons from the system'. *The* 'Technique of Rectal Irrigation' *in* 'The Knee-Chest Position' *is apparently best,* 'allowing from four to six pints of water to be injected safely and without inconvenience'. *He concludes:* 'Ponce de Léon may have been wrong in the notion that he could, perhaps, make his body live forever . . . but he was quite right in thinking that, when all was said and done, what he and the rest of the human race needed was a Bath.' *Macfadden, who was himself the author of* The Real Secret of Keeping Young, *enjoyed a long life, celebrating his 83rd birthday by parachuting into the Hudson River. He died of jaundice at the age of 87.*

The Romance of Leprosy
E. Mackerchar
The Mission to Lepers, 1949

> 'Even the intrepid enthusiast must falter on the threshold of such service.'
>   'All down the ages the disease of leprosy has fascinated writer, artist, and poet, providing each in turn with themes upon which to exercise the loftiest imagination, and the highest artistic skill.'

The heights of romance are to be found in the brief biography of Mrs Gong, the Chinese biblewoman of Foochow:

> 'Without the least fear of the disease this intrepid worker threw her whole soul and strength into the task allotted to her . . . the warning to avoid close contact with those to whom she ministered fell on deaf ears . . . Nine years passed and then the blow fell . . . "I never thought I would get it" was the pathetic remark of this brave sufferer.'

Grow Your Own Hair
Ron Maclaren
Glasgow: Healthway Publications, 1947

Living Canvas: A Romance of Aesthetic Surgery
Elisabeth Margetson
Methuen, 1936

From the Stump to the Limb
A. A. Marks
New York: A. A. Marks & Co., c.1890

An illustrated history and description of the artificial limb company, with testimonials: 'The hand you made and sent me was received in first class condition . . .'

My Prostate and Me
William Curtis Martin
New York: Cadell & Davies, 1994

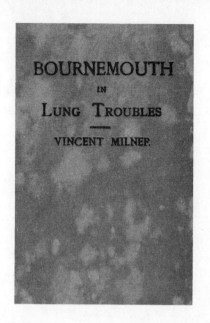

Bournemouth in Lung Troubles
Vincent Milner
Baillière, Tindall & Cox, 1896

First Report of the Standing Advisory Committee on Artificial Limbs
Ministry of Pensions, 1947

Acne at Your Fingertips
Tim Mitchell and Alison Dudley
Class Publishing, 2002

Psoriasis at Your Fingertips
Tim Mitchell, Rebecca Penzer and Jane Taylor
Class Publishing, 2000

Three Weeks in Wet Sheets
'A Moist Visitor to Malvern'
Hamilton, Adams & Co., 1856

Troubles We Don't Talk About
Joseph Franklin Montague
Philadelphia, PA: J. B. Lippincott Co., 1927

The troubles Montagu did not want to talk about were diseases of the rectum, but he was quite happy to discuss mal de mer, *as in his:*

Why Bring That Up? A Guide To and From Seasickness
New York: The Home Health Library, 1936

Coprology
Raymond A, Moody
Privately printed, 1972

'The art and science of character analysis, prognostication, and healing through the reading or manipulation of stools.'

Guts
John Edward Morton
Baltimore, MD: University Park Press, 1979

My Duodenal Ulcer and I
Dr Stuart Morton (pseudonym of John Spence Meighan)
Christopher Johnson, 1955

Electricity as a Cause of Cholera, or Other Epidemics, etc.
Sir James Murray
Dublin: J. M'Glashan, 1849

The Ethics of Medical Homicide and Mutilation
Austin O'Malley
New York: The Devin-Adair Co., 1922

A Treatise on the Virtues and Efficacy of the Saliva, or Fasting Spittle, Being Conveyed into the Intestines by Eating a Crust of Bread, Early in a Morning Fasting, in Relieving the Gout, Scurvey [sic], Gravel, Stone, Rheumatism, &c., Arising from Obstructions: Also, on the Great Cures Accomplished by the Fasting Spittle, When Externally Applied to Recent Cuts, Sore Eyes, Corns, Warts &c.
'A Physician'
Salem, MA: Henry Whipple, 1st American edition taken from 10th London edition, 1844

The Abuse of Elderly People:
A Handbook for Professionals
Jacki Pritchard
J. Kingsley, 1992

How to Get More Fun Out
of Smoking
Sidney P. Ram
Chicago, IL: Printed by Cuneo Press, 1941

Ashamed of My Arthritis
Lewis Rostron
Blackpool: The Author, 1965

'... I was forced to conclude that I had nothing wrong with me, originally, because I had the symptoms of everything, and that having the symptoms of everything I realised that I had nothing except the one big disease of modern diet ...'

Take a tin of soup, for instance: 'What have we at the end of it? A tin of fatty, flavoured water of negative value, with a one-way ticket on it to hospital ... ...'

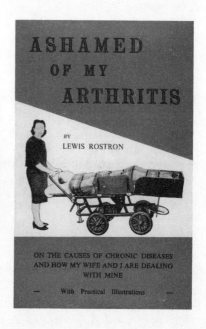

The World's Worst Teeth
Edward Samson
Staples Press, 1962

also the author of: **Art and the Full Prosthesis**
Heinemann, 1974

The Mesmeric Guide for Family Use
S. D. Saunders
H. Baillière, 1852

How to cure all known diseases by hypnotising your spouse, children, etc. Its fifty pages give concise instructions on curing deafness, cancer, consumption, and the common cold.

Backache, Birth and Figure Relief by Self-Revolving Hipbones
William Schoenau
Los Angeles, CA: The Author, 1951

Why Not Grow Young? or, ➤ Living for Longevity
Robert W. Service
Ernest Benn, 1928

'The writer wearing the costume in which he wrote this book.'

'There's comfort even in calamity, I concluded as I fingered my fifth muffin. Now let me take a gentle stroll to the cemetery and pick out a cosy corner. Or, how about a cheerful saunter to the crematorium?'

I Knew 3,000 Lunatics
Victor Robert Small
New York: Farrar & Rinehart, 1935

'I was privileged by fate and fortune to view from many angles the enactment of a complex drama of romance and comic pathos, and dark tragedy . . . and the theater wherein this drama was being enacted was an asylum for the insane; and the actors were the 3,000 lunatics confined therein . . . for six years I watched this show.'

How to Get Fat
Edward Smith
John Smith & Co., 1865

The Maniac. A Realistic Study of Madness from the Maniac's Point of View
E. Thelmar
Watts & Co., 1909

Two Health Problems – Constipation and Our Civilization
James Charles Thomson
Thorsons Publishers, 1943

'The connection between our Indigestion and our indecision; Our Food and our Behaviour. Advertising Specialists, Pain, Drugs and Enemas . . . I was discussing soured tissues with Henry Lynch, a Canadian engineer, at that time owner of the Marvel Cave in the Ozarks, Missouri, and also something of a biologist in his spare time . . .'

An Essay on Diseases Incidental to Literary and Sedentary Persons
Samuel Auguste André David Tissot
Printed for Edward & Charles Dilly, 1768

'It is universally known that there are books compos'd without any strength of genius, which appear quite insipid and unaffecting to the reader and only tire the eyes; but those that are compos'd with an exquisite force of ideas, and with an exact connexion of thought, elevate the soul, and fatigue it with the very pleasure which, the more compleat, lasting, and frequent it is, breaks the man the more . . . There is still living at Paris a professor of Rhetoric who fainted away whilst he was perusing some of the sublime passages of Homer. The head itself, and the nerves, and the stomach which is fuller of nerves than any other part, first suffer for the errors of the mind . . .'

Crook Frightfulness

'A Victim'
Birmingham: Cornish, 1932;
Birmingham: Moody Bros., revised
edition, 1935

*The author of this book, identified
only as 'A Victim', recounts the
story of his life as a rent collector
in the East End of London, in
New Zealand and the West Indies.*
Crook Frightfulness *is the
autobiography of a hunted man
who believes himself to be
continually hounded and molested
by evil men, or 'crooks'.*

'How was I to know that I had of my own volition opened the
doors of Hell – to turn me from a cheery, care-free youth of 18 to a
prematurely aged man, terrified by horrible men, threatening my
sanity and life?'

'I have had experiences which suggest crooks sometimes use a
stethoscope apparatus which enables them to hear your thoughts.'
He also provides a detailed account of what he describes as
'ventriloquial terrorism' *whereby* '. . . a molestor using
ventriloquism may be in a house or building or walking along in a
tram or bus or in a car, yet he can throw his voice anywhere
undetected by those who are near them.' *This technique gives rise to
various embarrassing experiences, including one where* 'I had just
bidden adieu to a friend on the Aberystwyth Marine Parade and had
just turned away from him when I heard the words – "The old sod"
– said in my voice tones too!"'

A Handbook of 'Chiropody' Giving the Causes and Treatment of Callosities, Bunions, Chilblains and the Diseases of the Toe-nails

Felix Wagner
Osborne, Garrett & Co., 1903

The 120-Year Diet: How to Double Your Vital Years

Roy L. Walford
New York: Simon & Schuster, 1986

Nasology; or, Hints Towards a Classification of Noses

Eden Warwick (pseudonym of George Jabet)
A. Bentley, 1848

Who's To Blame? or, A week's experience of a gastric follicle

William Michael Heaviside Whitmarsh
Henry Kimpton, 1874

'I was up betimes to look round and see if the work had been all finished over night, and to my surprise, I found it had not. Mutton parcels were lying here, apple ditto there, whilst small packages of nuts were everywhere. I discovered most of my comrades asleep, being done up I suppose by the irregular hours . . . Master . . . had caught a cold . . . took some very hot tea . . . which we duly received, the tea being so hot it nearly scalded some of my younger brethren . . .'

Clinical Hat Pegs for Students and Graduates

Robert Joseph Willan
Heinemann, 1951

Natural Bust Enlargement with Total Mind Power: How to Use the Other 90 Per Cent of Your Mind to Increase the Size of Your Breasts

Donald L. Wilson

Larkspur, CA: Total Mind Power Institute, 1979

Synthetic Mania. By the author of 'Certified'. An Autobiographical Study

H. G. Woodley

Pen-In-Hand Publishing Co., 1948

'Madness is universal . . .'

'This book follows up his two previous works in which he describes his certification and confinement in a Mental Asylum for over a year. He puts forward a possible cause of insanity.'

'The mind of each was so centred upon the sex organ of the other, that it was neither the time nor the place to expect them to see any connection between their behaviour and that of the individual who plays golf with a buttercup . . . nor did they see that their behaviour was in full accord with the theories of the Marquis de Sade . . . Perhaps some day, they would understand these things, who can tell . . .'

Moles and their Meaning.
With regard to the Mind,
Morals and Astral Indications
in Both Sexes, Being a
Modernised and Easy Guide
to the Ancient Science of
Divination by the Moles of
the Human Body (Founded
on the Works and Researches
of one Richard Sanders, A.D.
1653, and Other Eminent
Astrologers of About the
Same Period)
Harry de Windt
C. Arthur Pearson, 1907

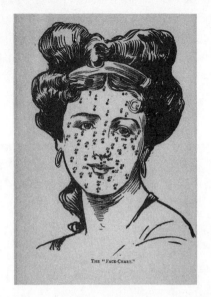

THE "FACE-CHART."

The Diagnosis of the Acute Abdomen in Rhyme
'Zeta' (pseudonym of Sir Vincent Zachary Cope)
H. K. Lewis, 1947

'The leading or principal symptoms are four,
They often are fewer and but seldom more . . .
The "big" four I mention whom you must watch well
More clearly the site of their author to tell
Come right off the tongue in a simple refrain –
Distension, rigidity, vomiting, pain.'

10
SEX & MARRIAGE

Seven Wives and Seven Prisons; or, Experiences in the Life of a Matrimonial Monomaniac. A True Story Written by Himself
L. A. Abbott
New York: The Author, 1870

The frontispiece portrait is of 'My first and worst wife'.

MY FIRST AND WORST WIFE

Shipping Semen? How to Have a Successful Experience
Pennie Ahmed
Sun City, CA: Winlock Publishing Co., 1998

Sex in Industry
Azel Ames
Boston, MA: J. R. Osgood, 1875

Love, Woman, Marriage: the Grand Secret
Anon.
Boston, MA: Randolph Publishing Co., 1871

'No description, critique, or synopsis can do justice to this mighty work, which ought to be bound in gold and be on the table of every man, woman and youth in the land and in the world. It is an exhaustive and large work.'

Onania; or, The Heinous Sin of Self-Pollution, and all its Frightful Consequences, in Both Sexes, Considered

Anon.
The Author, 1725; 19th edition, 1759

The Secret Companion, a Medical Work on Onanism

'The Authors'
R. J. Brodie & Co., 1845

Literature of Kissing

Charles C. Bombaugh
Philadelphia, PA: J. B. Lippincott, 1876

> 'Who was it caught me when I fell
> And Kissed the place to make it well?
> My mother.'
>
> 'Catch the white-handed nymphs in shady places,
> And woo sweet kisses from averted faces.'
>
> 'The overture kiss to the opera of love.'
>
> 'Life's autumnal blossoms fall
> And death's brown clinging lips impress
> The long cold kiss that waits us all.'

Sex + Sex = Gruppensex

Ruediger Bosschmann
Flensburg: Stephenson Verlag, 1970

Bosschmann was also the author of:

Orgasmus und Super-Orgasmus
Flensburg: Stephenson Verlag, 1972

Sexual Analysis of Dickens' Props

Arthur Washburn Brown
New York: Emerson Books, 1971

'A work inspired by Susanna Nobbe.'

Chapters include:
Why Cribbage Represents Sexual Intercourse
The Erotic Meaning of Wooden Legs
Erotic Umbrellas and Sexually Suggestive Food
Beanstalk Country: On Top of the Tallest Erection
The Drowned Man's Little Finger
How to Bring the Phallus back from the Dead

SEXUAL ANALYSIS OF

𝕯𝕴𝕮𝕶𝕰𝕹𝕾' 𝕻𝕽𝕺𝕻𝕾

ARTHUR WASHBURN BROWN

Is the Pleasure Worth the Penalty? A Common-sense View of the Leading Vice of the Age

Henry Butter
Job Caudwell, 1866

Castration: The Advantages and the Disadvantages

Victor T. Cheney
Bloomington, IN: AuthorHouse, 2003

How to Speak and Write to Girls for Friendship

B. A. Chinaka
Onitsha: Njoku & Sons Bookshop, c.1963

Notes Sur la Sodomie

Jean Paul Henry Coutagne
Lyons: H. Georg, 1880

Women Around Hitler

Randolph S. Davies

E. Newman, Know Thine Enemy series, c.1943

Publisher's description: 'This is a real thriller. It is a story which recalls mediaeval life, loves, intrigues and murders in the dark passages of castles . . . well illustrated' *(i.e.: one drawing).*

'One of his women, when asked why her friendship with Hitler came to an end, said that she had a disappointment with him which did not redound to his advantage.'

How to Pick Up Women in Discos

Don Diebel

Houston, TX: Gemini Publishing Co., 1981

The Girdle of Chastity

Eric John Dingwall

George Routledge & Sons, 1931

The definitive book on chastity belts.

Straight Talk About Surgical Penis Enlargement

Gary M. Griffin

Los Angeles, CA: Added Dimensions, 1993

Encyclopaedia of Sexual Knowledge

Norman Haire (ed.), A. Costler and A. Willy (both pseudonyms)
Encyclopaedic Press, 1934

Fig. C-15—Picture story of various causes for sexual excitation and erection.

How they act on the erection center of the medulla, which issues the "order" for an erection through the erector nerves.

How To Be Happy Though Married

Rev. Edward J. Hardy
T. Fisher Unwin, 1885

'To those brave men and women who have ventured, or intend to venture, into that state which is "a blessing to a few, a curse to many, and a great uncertainty to all", this book is dedicated in admiration of their courage.'

How to Pick Up More Girls

Rory Harrity
Modern Age, 1972

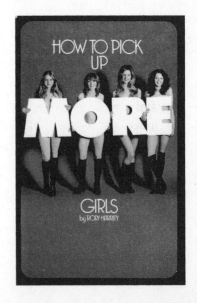

Wed To a Lunatic. A Wild, Weird Yarn of Love and Some Other Things Delivered in the Form of Hash for the Benefit of Tired Readers

Frank Warren Hastings ('Author of several widely unknown works')
St. Johnsbury, VT: L. W. Rowell, 1896

The second edition was retitled:

Wed To a Lunatic. A Lie.

St. Johnsbury, VT: The Caledonian Press, 1901

The Madam as Entrepreneur: Career Management in House Prostitution
Barbara Sherman Heyl
New Brunswick, NJ: Transaction Books, 1979

The Population of Great Britain Broken Down by Age & Sex
HMSO, 1991

Celtic Sex Magic: For Couples, Groups and Solitary Practitioners
Jon G. Hughes
Rochester, VT: Destiny Books, 2001

Male Sexuality: The Atlantis Position
Jenny James
Caliban Books, 1982

External Genitalia of Japanese Females
Kanji Kasai
Tokyo: Free Press, 1995

In 26 years of practice, Dr Kasai examined the genitalia of over 10,000 Japanese women and features 8,330 of them in this statistical and photographic survey.

Sexual Health for Men: The 'At Your Fingertips' Guide
Philip Kell and Vanessa Griffiths
Class Publishing, 2003

Penis Sheaths and their Distribution in Africa
Sture Lagercrantz
Uppsala: Uppsala University, 1976

Venereal Disease and Its Prevention
Felix Raoul Leblanc
Letchworth: G. W. Browne, 1920
'To my wife this book is affectionately dedicated.'

Training of the Young in Laws of Sex
Hon. Edward Lyttelton
Longman, 1900

'Strength of appetite' *in a child of ten or eleven suggests, according to the author, that* 'physical temptation later will be very strong'. *This is the only sure symptom that a boy is* 'contracting the habit'.

Be Married and Like It
Bernarr Macfadden
New York: Macfadden Book Co., 1937

Macfadden was also the author of:

How Can I Get Married?
New York: Macfadden Publications, 1927

Subtitled 'A Woman Bares Her Soul: Vividly and Dramatically she tells the Story of her Heart-Stirring Experience in her Search for a Husband.'

and:

A Strenuous Lover: A Romance of a Natural Love's Vast Power
New York: Physical Culture Publishing Co., 1904

and:

The Power and Beauty of Superb Womanhood. How they are Lost and How they May be Regained
New York: Physical Culture Publishing Co., 1901

and:

The Virile Powers of Superb Manhood. How developed, how lost: how regained
Bernarr A. Macfadden
New York: Physical Culture Publishing Co., 1900

> 'That horrible curse MASTURBATION. Vitality has an enemy
> with which it literally has no chance. When a boy finally escapes
> from the clutches of this Gorgon evil, he is cursed with night losses
> that waste his vitality almost as speedily and then is confronted with
> promiscuous intercourse. This habit is not practised long without
> severe suffering. Then the torture of body and mind is terrible.
> Though many fall by the wayside, the majority get through with
> enough vital and sexual strength to look with favor on marriage.
> The girl that such a man marries is usually weak . . . then sexual
> excess brings its frightful ravages on the physical man. This sexual
> excess continues until impotence intervenes. There you have the life
> of the average civilised man.'

Race Making: A few suggestions to women on the importance of their work in Race Making

Mrs David MacConnel
Health For All Publishing Co., 1927

> 'Early fertilization makes for female and late for male . . . A woman
> must take the onus . . . tie a piece of ribbon – blue is a good colour
> because it means sincerity – on the bed head and when it is there
> "times are not convenient".'

In and Out and Up and Down

Jo L. G. McMahon
New York: John Martin's Book House, 1922

History of The Girls' Friendly Society

Agnes L. Money
Gardner, Darton & Co., 1897

The Breathless Orgasm: A Lovemap Biography of Asphyxiophilia

John Money, Gordon Wainwright and David Hinsburger
Buffalo, NY: Prometheus Books, 1991

What Women Are Thinking About Men

J. O. Nnadozie

Onitsha, Nigeria: Confidence Printing Press, J. C. Brothers Bookshop, n.d.

'All lovers of truth, and impartial observer would agree with me that our women do not play "LOVE" in its natural way.

They love to kick boys like football. All they think always is how to trick a man.

No. 1. Bomb to women by Mr Emmanuel Eze, the Woman Challenger.

Women are liars and great deceivers. When they tell you yes, they mean no. Those men who used them as pillows are sleeping on hard stone.

Some of them are money mongers. They like money as monkey likes bananas.

Please men, know yourselves for some women are very dangerous. If you are not careful you become useless. Things of nowadays are very hard.'

High-Performance Stiffened Structures

Anon.

Bury St Edmunds: PEP, 2000

The Sex Practitioner: a Step by Step Guide to the Pleasures of Sex

Harry Prick

New York: I. M. Horny, 1945

According to the National Union Catalog, there is only one recorded copy of this title (in the library of the University of Oregon, Eugene). Harry Prick is a leading authority on the Dutch author Lodewijk van Deyssel.

Heroic Virgins
Alfonso P. Santos
Quezon City, Philippines: National Book Store, 1977

The Causes of Infidelity Removed
Rev. Stephen Smith
Utica, NY: Grosh & Hutchinson, 1839

How to Pick Up Girls on Public Beaches
Raleigh Leo Stanley
Great Neck, NY: Todd & Honeywell, 1982

Bullying and Sexual Harassment: A Practical Handbook
Tina Stephens and Jane Hallas
Oxford: Chandos Publishing, 2006

Syphilis: or, A Poetical History of the French Disease
N. Tate (translator)
For Jacob Tonson, 1686

The English translation of Girolamo Fracastoro's Syphilis sive morbus Gallicus *(Verona: n.p., 1530) – the book that gave us the word 'syphilis'.*

Sex and the Athlete
Charles T. Trevor
The Mitre Press, 1946

'First of all let me say that I am no authority on sex . . . so vast indeed are the varying facets of this absorbing subject that one would need to make it a life study . . . The importance of sex knowledge to the man in training need not be emphasised, for hundreds of would-be champions have known defeat through this one factor.'

SEX — AND THE ATHLETE

A Frank Exposition of Sane Sexology as it effects the Athlete and Health Culturist from Infancy to Old Age

By CHAS. T. TREVOR

SECOND REVISED EDITION

PRICE 2/- NETT

Published by—
THE MITRE PRESS, MITRE CHAMBERS, MITRE STREET, E.C.3

Sex Efficiency through Exercises
Th. H. Van der Velde
Heinemann, 1933

Sex & Money
The Warden of the Order of Silence
Kensington: The Settlement Press, n.d.

> '. . . all the troubles of human life can be grouped under one or other of these two words.'

Vital Force; or, Evils and Remedies of Perverted Sexuality. Shewing how the health, strength, energy, and beauty of human beings are wasted and how preserved
R. B. D. Wells ('Practical Phrenologist of Observatory Villa, West Bank, Scarborough')
Oldham: H. Vickers, & Co., 1878

> 'Nicotine powerfully affects the brain, and the cerebellum which is the seat of the affections, becomes congested or inflamed; this in turn irritates the genital parts, produces sexual excitability, and conduces to masturbation. This latter in turn draws the blood and electricity from the brain and other parts of the body to the genital organs, and creates an abnormal craving for something which neither food nor natural drink can appease.'

A Kiss for a Blow
Henry Clarke Wright
Milner & Co., n.d.

Happy Though Married
Sophia Gertrude Wurtz
n.p., n.d. [c.1922]

11
KEEP-FIT

Mechanical Exercise A Means of Cure, Being a Description of the Zander Institute, London: Its History, Appliances, Scope and Object. Edited by the Medical Officer to the Institution
Anon.
J. & A. Churchill, 1883

An astonishing collection of machines designed to exercise one part of the body at a time, including 'Abduction' *of the legs.*

How to Pose as a Strong Man
W. Barton-Wright
Pearson's Magazine, *1899*

'How, when lying at length on two chair backs placed at your extremities, to support a person standing on your chest.'

Text-book of Club Swinging
Tom Burrows
Health and Strength, *1908*

Ball Punching
Tom Carpenter
Athletic Publications, 1923
'World's Champion All-round Ball-Puncher'

The Man with the Iron Eyebrows
Edouard Charles
Royal Magazine, *1902*

Mr Gregor Olivos '. . . screws his eyebrows between the two horizontal steel bars of the apparatus, enabling him to lift 244 lbs.'

Strenuous Americans
Roy Floyd Dibble
New York: Boni & Liveright, 1923

Jogging – The Dance of Death
Robert Gene Fineberg
Port Washington, NY: Ashley Books, 1984

Ten Minutes' Exercise for Busy Men
Luther Gulick
British Sports Publishing Co., 1906

The Big Chest Book
Bob Hoffman
York, PA: Strength & Health Publishing Co., 1950

The Culture of the Abdomen, the Cure of Obesity and Constipation ➤
F. A. Hornibrook
Heinemann, 1924

A classic that went to 11 editions between 1924 and 1937, cured Arnold Bennett of dyspepsia and gave H. G. Wells 'a new lease of life'.

Massage and the Original Swedish Movements
Kurre W. Ostrom
H. K. Lewis, 1912 (7th edition)

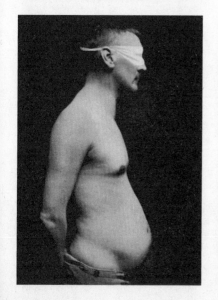

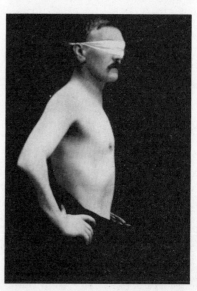

Fitness For All with the Wonder Ball
Edi Polz
Odhams Press, 1938

Described on the titlepage as 'The famous physical culture expert of international reputation', *Edi Polz's entire repertoire consists of routines performed with his 'Wonder Ball', an object approximately the size of a cricket ball, but with protuberances that make it look like a miniature marine mine. Whether the man and woman who demonstrate his range of exercises are walking, lying down, or even diving into a pool, the ubiquitous Wonder Ball is brought into play.*

Scientific Bag Punching
Harry Seeback
New York: Richard K. Fox, 1905

Pray Your Weight Away
Charlie W. Shedd
Philadelphia PA: Lippincott, 1957

Exercise in the Bath ➤
Turillo Ristori Togna
Putnam, 1938

JARM – How To Jog with your Arms to Live Longer
Joseph D. Wassersug
Port Washington, NY: Ashley Books, 1983

Exercises for Athletes
F. A. M. Webster and J. A. Heys
John F. Shaw, 1932

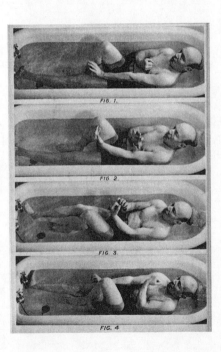

FIG. 1.

FIG. 2.

FIG. 3.

FIG. 4.

12
SPORT

Pole Stars. Some Extraordinary Performances on a Pole
H. L. Adam
n.p., 1902

Featuring De Witt and Burns, 'Perch Equilibrists', performing on a mast 100 feet high.

How to Twirl a Baton
Anon.
Chicago, IL: Ludwig & Ludwig, c.1930

How to Walk
Anon.
Evening News, *1903*

Wrestling for Gay Guys
Donald Black
Power Books, 1994

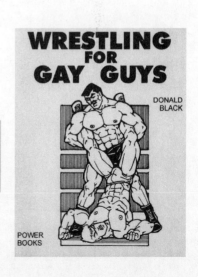

'For those thinking about taking up wrestling – whether for fun, fitness, self-defence, safe expression of anger or erotic stimulation.'

Athletics for Politicians
Sir Charles W. Dilke
Athenaeum Press, 1900

Green Memory of Days with Gun and Rod
J. B. Drought
Philip Allan, 1937
Dedicated to '. . . the best bag I ever made in Ireland – My Wife.'

Queen Victoria and Ping-pong
Gwendolen Freeman (ed.)
Studley; Brewin Books, 2004

By His Own Hand: A Study of Cricket's Suicides
David Frith
Stanley Paul, 1991
More than 80 examples of cricketers who have killed themselves.

Myself & My Boxers
Jack Goodwin
Hutchinson, 1924

Squid Jiggling from Small Boats
Mototsugu Hamabe, et al.
Fishing News Books, 1989

How You Can Bowl Better Using Self-hypnosis
Jack Heise
Hollywood, CA: Wilshire Book Co,, 1961

The New 'Soccer' Football Game
Ho-Mo
n.p., 1932

New Sensations for Horse & Rider
Tanya Larrigan
J. A. Allen, 2000
Foreword by Sir Paul McCartney

Side and Screw, Being Notes on the Theory and Practice of the Game of Billiards
Charles Dealtry Locock
Longmans, 1901

Knight Life: Jousting in the United States
Robert L. Loeffelbein
Lexington Park, MD: Golden Owl, 1978

Fancy Cycling: Trick Riding for Amateurs
Isabel Marks
Sands & Co., 1901

Knife Throwing: A Practical Guide
Harry K. McEvoy
Rutland, VT: Charles E. Tuttle Co., 1973

The Unwritten Laws of Fox-Hunting. Notes on the Use of the Horn and the Whistle, and List of 5,000 Names of Hounds
C. F. P. McNeill
Vinton & Co., 1911

Rope Spinning
D. W. Pinkney
Herbert Jenkins, 1930

Racing Axemen: A History of Competitive Woodchopping in Australia
J. Preston
Melbourne: Hawthorn, 1980

Jerks In From Short Leg
'Quid' (pseudonym of Robert Allan Fitzgerald)
Harrison, 1866

Fun on the Billiard Table

'Stancliffe'
C. Arthur Pearson, 1899

He was also the author of:

The Autobiography of a Caddy-Bag
Methuen, 1924

Play With Your Own Marbles

J. J. Wright
S. W. Partridge, c.1865

'While Dick knelt down, ready to fire, Syl could not help but clutch his wonderfully-got bag of marbles all the tighter.'

13

LEISURE

Collect Fungi on Stamps
D. J. Aggersberg
Gibbons, 1997

How to Vamp Without Music
Anon.
J. F. Dallas, 1943

Ten Good Tricks With Empty Bass Bottles
Anon.
Burton-on-Trent: Bass, Ratcliff & Gretton, 1929

Hypnotism and Suggestion ➤
Edwin Ash
J. Jacobs, 1906

By means of the hypnoscope, the practitioner can achieve: 'Tetanic Catalepsy . . . a fixation of the limbs . . . the whole body may be made as rigid as a steel bar so that it may be rested with the head on one chair and the feet on another, and heavy weights placed on it . . . After a few experiments this steel-like catalepsy can be produced in even the feeblest people.'

The Great Pantyhose Crafts Book
Ed and Stevie Baldwin
New York: Western Publishing Co., Inc., 1982

This book gives patterns for forty different articles that can be made from old tights, starting with 'gifts and bazaar [*sic*] items for everyone'.

'Little Black Evening Bag – If you've always admired the evening purses in the stores but hated to spend the money, then this project is for you!'

'The perfect touch . . . for your home décor' *can be created in the shape of a life-size stuffed* "granny", *and* 'shady lady', *while the pantyhose cactus* 'is sure to be a conversation piece . . . requiring 'even less care than a real one.'

Master Pieces: Making Furniture from Paintings
Richard Ball and Peter Campbell
Poole: Blandford, 1983

Practical Taxidermy and Home Decoration
Joseph H. Batty
New York: Orange Judd, 1880

Chess Endings for Beginners
J. H. Blake (ed.)
Routledge, 1900

Inkle Weaving
Lavinia Bradley
Routledge, 1982

Indian Conjuring
Maj. L. H. Branson
Routledge, 1922

'I dedicate this small volume to my wife who has always been my best audience and my keenest critic at the innumerable sleight-of-hand performances that I have had the pleasure of giving in her presence.'

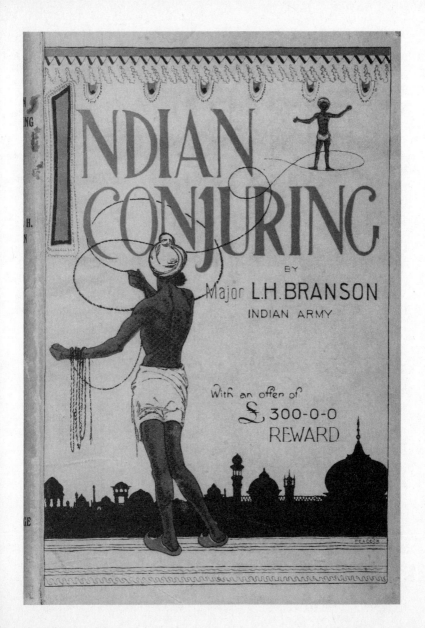

INDIAN CONJURING

BY

Major L.H. BRANSON

INDIAN ARMY

With an offer of

£ 300-0-0
REWARD

Amusing Yourself with Paper and String: Learn How to Pass a Person Through a Bus Ticket and Many Other Wizard Accomplishments

Paul Bruton
Universal Publications, c.1938

Practical Candle Burning

Raymond Buckland
St. Paul, MN: Llewellyn Publications, 1970

Pranks with the Mouth

W. C.
Chamber's Journal, *1879*

Pleasant Work for Busy Fingers

Maggie Browne
Cassell, 1896

Sharpened Tools for Busy Workers

John Sweet Doidge
James Nisbet, 1897

Proceedings of the Second International Potato Modeling Conference

A. J. Haverkort and D. K. L. MacKerron (eds.)
Dordrecht: Kluwer Academic Publishers, 1995

The Champion Orange Peeler

A. B. Henn
Strand, *1899*

The author, a ship's cook, demonstrates how to make extraordinary patterns, faces, crowns, animals, and pyramids out of orange peel.

Suggestive Thoughts for Busy Workers
J. Osborne Keen
Bible Christian Book Room, 1883

Learn to Croon
Brand Larkin
W. Foulsham & Co., 1936

Fun with Boxes
Joseph Leeming
New York: Frederick A. Stokes Co., 1937

Crocheting Novelty Pot-holders
L. Macho
New York: Dover, 1982

Woodcarving with a Chainsaw
Lyn Mangan
Kenthurst, NSW: Kangaroo Press, 1997

Knitted Historical Figures
Jan Messent
Search Press, 1992

Levitation for Terrestrials
Robert Kingley Morison (ed.)
Ascent, 1977

Suggestive Handwork for Lower Classes
Arthur B. Neal
Pitman, 1874

Searching for Railway Telegraph Insulators
W. Keith Neal
St Saviours, Guernsey: The Signal Box Press, 1982
and its sequel:

Railway and Other Rare Insulators
St Saviours, Guernsey: The Signal Box Press, 1987

Frolic and Fun with Egg-Shells

Meredith Nugent

Girl's Realm, 1903

> **'**After trying some of the schemes here suggested, you will find the fun is not only rollicking, but well nigh inexhaustible.**'**

Nugent was also the author of:

How to Have Fun with Old Newspapers

Girl's Realm, 1903

You Can Make a Stradivarius Violin

Joseph V. Reid

Chicago, IL: Popular Mechanics Press, 1950 and 1955

Mr Reid was an engineer employed by the American Can Company of Canada. 'With experience anyone can make two violins a year and still play golf and fish.'

Build Your Own Hindenburg

Alan Rose

New York: Putnam, 1983

Spirit Rapping Made Easy

Dion Sweird

Felix McGlennan, 1926

Explosive Spiders & How to Make Them

John Scoffern

Boy's Own Paper, 1881

Pyrotechnicist Scoffern shows how to manufacture an '. . . artificial spider that, when touched, should go off with a bang.'

Scoffern was also author of:

Firework Pie for a Picnic

Boy's Own Paper, 1882

14
CLOTHES & FASHION

Why She Should Start Wearing a Bra
Anon.
Kayser Bondor Research Bureau, n.d.

Shoe Bottom Costing
E. S. Bream
The British Boot, Shoe and Allied Trades Research Association, 1936

Some Fact and Fallacies in Connection with the Trade in Fancy Feathers
C. F. Downham
London Chamber of Commerce, 1910

Intemperance and Tight Lacing, Considered in Relation to the Laws of Life
O. S. Fowler
Wortley: J. Watson, printed by Joseph Barker, 1849

'Let the finger of scorn be pointed at every tight-laced woman, and let tight waists be shunned . . . The practice is disgraceful, is immoral, is *murderous*; for it is gradual *suicide*, and almost certain *infanticide*.'

Let's Make Some Undies
Marion Hall
W. Foulsham & Co., 1954

The Art of Chapeaugraphy
John G. Hamley
C. Routledge, 1923

The Romance of Rayon
Arnold Henry Hard
Manchester: Whittaker & Robinson, 1933

Making It in Leather
M. Vincent Hayes
New York: Drake, 1972; Newton Abbot: David & Charles, 1973

Prehistoric Sandals from Northeastern Arizona
Kelley Ann Hays-Gilpin, et al.
Tucson, AZ: University of Arizona Press, 1998

Living without Gloves
Halford E. Luccock
Oxford: Oxford University Press, 1957

Parish Ministers' Hats
James Martin
Chapter House Ltd, 1997

The Leather Slapper
Nelson Coral Nye
Nicholson & Watson, 1937

Men Dressed as Seamen
Samuel Gorley Putt
Christophers, 1943

A History of Victorian Skirt Grips
Mary Sawdon
Cambridge: Midsummer Books, 1995

Hours and Earnings in the Leather-glove Industry
Rebecca Glover Smaltz
Washington, DC: United States Government Printing Office, 1934

15
FOOD & DRINK

The Life and Cuisine of Elvis Presley
David Adler
New York: Crown, 1993

How to Eat a Peanut
Anon.
New York: n.p., c.1900

How to Make Pastry Attractive
Anon.
Van Den Berghs & Jurgens, n.d.

The New Radiation Recipe Book
Anon.
New World, c.1930

'Household hints and useful information, together with a selection of tested recipes with the suitable Regulo marks and cooking times appended, for use with the New World Regulo-controlled Gas Cookers and Ranges.'

Various editions of the 'Radiation Cookery Book' were in print between 1920 and 1968.

Report of the Temperature Reached in Army Biscuits During Baking, Especially with Reference to the Destruction of the Imported Flour-Moth Ephestia Kuhnelia Zeller
Anon.
Journal of the Royal Army Medical Corps, *1913*

The Romance of Tea

Anon.

English and Scottish Joint Co-operative Wholesale Society, 1934

Some Interesting Facts about Margarine

Anon.

n.p., n.d.

Be Bold with Bananas

Banana Control Board

Pretoria: Muller & Retief, 1970

Faulty Bread

W. T. Banfield

The British Baker, 1939

Possible 'faults' include:
- Wrong weight
- Lack of volume
- Lack of crust colour
- Excessive crust colour
- Blisters
- Flying tops and ugly bursts
- Crust shell loose and cracking surfaces
- Lack of oven-spring and external shred
- Rough crust surfaces
- Unpleasant aromas and tastes
- Bad buttering surfaces
- Poor crumb colours
- Irregular streaky textures
- Large holes and slits
- Clammy bread
- Cores and seams
- Unusual colours

Frog Raising for Pleasure and Profit

Dr Albert Broel
New Orleans, LA: Marlboro House, 1950

Broel, the 'Originator of Canned Frog Legs', *provides recipes, including:*

Baked Apples stuffed with Giant Frog Meat

Wash and core six red apples, scoop pulp from centers, and cook until thick with 1 tablespoon melted butter. Add one can of Giant Bullfrog Meat, shredded and blend well. Stuff apples. Garnish tops with buttered breadcrumbs and bake until apples are tender in medium oven. Serve hot.

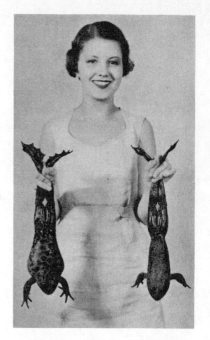

Giant Bullfrog Fondue

Grate 1/2 lb. of Switzerland cheese and melt on fire with: 1 tablespoon butter. Beat 2 eggs with one cup cream, salt to taste and add to cheese mixture, stirring constantly, then add 1 1/2 cup of chopped Giant Bullfrog cooked meat and mix well. Let simmer on fire 5 minutes or until mixture is thick and serve on toast. You may garnish with slices of hard boiled eggs.

10,000 Snacks

Cora, Rose and Bob Brown
Garden City, NY: Halcyon House, 1948
'Of snacks there is no end.'

Eating in Two or Three Languages

Irvin S. Cobb
Hodder & Stoughton, 1919

Detecting Foreign Bodies in Food
M. Edwards (ed.)
Woodhead Publishing, 2004

Cameos of Vegetarian Literature
Charles W. Forward (ed.)
The Ideal Publishing Union, 1898
Vegetarian Jubilee Library Vol. VIII
Includes 'The Slaughter of Animals for Food' by Henry S. Salt,
and 'The Turnip in Sickness and Health' by Doris Y. Pepper.

How I Lived on 4³/₄d. a Day. By a Woman Who Now Realizes that She has Hitherto Eaten too Much
Janetta Griffiths Foulkes
Truslove & Bray, c.1912

Pernicious Pork; or, Astounding Revelations of the Evil Effects of Eating Swine Flesh
William T. Hallett
New York: Broadway Publishing Co., 1903

Ice Cream for Small Plants
Etta H. Handy
Chicago, IL: Hotel Monthly Press, 1937

The History of the Melton Mowbray Pork Pie
Trevor Hickman
Stroud, Sutton Publishing, 2005

The Complete Book of Bacon
William J. Hogan
Northwood Books, 1978

Why Not Eat Insects?
Vincent M. Holt
Field & Tuer, 1885

Menu

Snail Soup
Fried Soles, with Woodlouse Sauce
Curried Cockchafers
Fricassée of Chicken with Chrysalids
Boiled Neck of Mutton with Wireworm Sauce
Cauliflowers garnished with Caterpillars
Moths on Toast

Food for Survival After a Disaster. With Plates
Raymond Charles Hutchinson
Carlton: Melbourne University Press, 1959

Dainty Dishes for Slender Incomes
'Isobel' of *Home Notes*
C. Arthur Pearson, 1895

Modest fare: 'Turbot in Lobster Sauce', 'Duck and Salad',
'Soles à la Normande' and 'Grouse and Chips'.

About Raw Juices
John B. Lust
New York: Benedict Lust Publications, 1982

Salted Peanuts: 1800 Little Known Facts
E. C. McKenzie
Grand Rapids, MI: Baker Book House, 1972

How to Cook Roadkill: Gourmet Cooking
Richard Marcou
Publishers' Group West, 1987

The Thermodynamics of Pizza

Harold J. Morowitz

New Brunswick, NJ: Rutgers University Press, 1991

What Can I Do with my Juicer?

Barbara Norman

New York: Bantam, 1992

Dangerous Cocoa; or, The Perils of Kola

'Quaesitor'

James Hutcheson Hogg, 1898

Cold Meat and How to Disguise It

Mrs M. E. Rattray

C. Arthur Pearson, 1904

What To Do with Cold Mutton: A Book of Réchauffés

Mary Renny

Richard Bentley & Son, 1863

Tommy Apple and his Adventures in Banana-Land

Henry Rox and James Laver

Jonathan Cape, 1935

Miss Smallwood's Goodies. Easy Sweetmeat Making at Home

M. Smallwood

Manchester: The Author, 2nd edition, c.1890

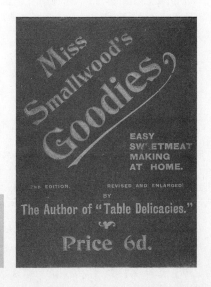

'If food is the way to a man's heart, there is no doubt that any man would want to get his hands on Miss Smallwood's Goodies.'

Soyer's Paper-Bag Cookery
Nicolas Soyer
Andrew Melrose, 1911

By the grandson of 'the great Soyer'. After experimenting with various sorts of paper which tainted the flavour of the cooked food, Messrs. James Spicer & Sons manufactured a paper 'which met all my requirements'. *So,* 'with Paper-Bag Cookery there is no likelihood of an imperfectly cooked joint. There will be no pots or pans to clean; the drudgery of the kitchen will be abolished'. *Soyer was chef at Brooks's Club; his rival C. Herman Senn of The Reform Club also published* The Paper-Bag Cookery Manual *in the same year – promoting the bag sponsored by the* Express *newspaper, the* Papakuk.

Living Without Eating
Herbert Thurston
Reprinted from The Month, *1931*

Among the feats of 'famous fasting girls' *described by Mr Newman are the* '. . . five years' unbroken fast by Therese Neumann of Konnersreuth, Bavaria'.

How to Cook Husbands
Elizabeth Strong Worthington
New York: Dodge Publishing Co., 1899

and:

The Gentle Art of Cooking Wives
New York: Dodge Publishing Co., 1900

How to Survive Snack Attacks Naturally
Shari and Judi Zucker
Santa Barbara, CA: Woodbridge Press Publishing Co., 1979

16

TRANSPORT & TOURISM

Progressive Afghanistan
Mohammad Ali
Lahore: Punjab Educational Electric Press, 1933

'My object in writing this book is to show how the famished and bankrupt Afghan nation was rescued from utter ruin and annihilation and brought once more on to the path of progress . . . the exhausted and war-weary tribes of Afghanistan have been transformed within a surprisingly short period into a living and powerful nation . . . The country has not only recovered from the severe set-back sustained by internecine war, but is also advancing rapidly in social and economic sphere. . . The people are happy and contented. After several years of stress and strain they are now able to enjoy perfect peace and to look forward to a bright future.'

More than 50 years on, Mr Ali's optimism was continued by:

Afghanistan. A Nation in Love with Freedom
Abdul Hakim Tabibi
Cedar Rapids, IA: Igram Press, 1985

Bike-Riders Aids
Anon.
The Holdsworthy Co., c.1950

Kinki Tourists' Guide

Anon.

n.p., c.1960

'Kinki Women Make World's Best Wives.'

Through Holland on Skates

Anon.

Association for the Promotion of Home and Foreign Travel, 1894

Weymouth, the English Naples

Anon.

Middlesbrough: Hood & Co., 1910

'Go to Weymouth. There you will find pure air, pure water, warm sunshine, bright sea, sweet sloping pebbly beaches, firm fine sands, good bathing, boating, yachting, cycling, golfing, etc. The distance from London is 142½ miles, and the journey takes a few minutes over three hours.'

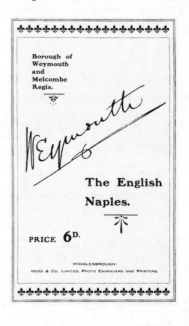

Why People Move

Jorge Balan (ed.)

Paris: UNESCO, 1981

Life and Laughter 'midst the Cannibals

Clifford Whiteley Collinson

Hurst & Blackett, 1926

Relates the story of a sailor visiting the Solomon Islands who avoided being eaten by cannibals but whose false teeth fell overboard; in attempting to retrieve them, he was eaten alive by a shark.

Recollections of Squatting in Victoria
Edward Micklethwaite Curr
Melbourne: George Robertson, 1883

Versailles: The View from Sweden
Elaine Evans Dee and Guy Walton
New York: Cooper-Hewitt Museum, 1988

How to Save a Big Ship From Sinking, Even Though Torpedoed
Charles V. A. Eley
Simpkin, Marshall & Co., 1915

The cover illustration shows a ship in a vertical position. It turns out to be the Titanic, *the caption inside reading, 'And she did eventually attain the perpendicular'.*

Round the World on a Wheel
John Foster Fraser
Methuen, 1904

Five Thousand Miles on a Sledge
Lionel F. Gowing
Chatto & Windus, 1889

A Thousand Miles on an Elephant
Holt Samuel Hallett
Edinburgh: Blackwood & Sons, 1890

Locomotive Boiler Explosions
Christian H. Hewison
Newton Abbot: David & Charles, 1983

'Always engrossing . . . sometimes disturbing.'
(Book club advertisement)

To Lake Tanganyika in a Bath Chair
Annie Boyle Hore
Sampson, Low & Co., 1886

A Wizard's Wanderings from China to Peru
John Watkins Holden
Dean & Sons, 1886

Quiet Wind Assisted Cycle Routes
Richard N. Hutchins
Clapham, Bedford: The Author, 1995

Gay Bulgaria
Stowers Johnson
Robert Hale, 1964
Once noted in a survey as the least borrowed book in British libraries.

Teach Yourself Air Navigation
'Kaspar'
The English Universities Press, 1942

Was Oderic of Pordenone Ever in Tibet?
Berthold Laufer
n.p., 1914

In Dwarf Land and Cannibal Country
Albert Bushnell Lloyd
T. Fisher Unwin, 1899

Flights of Fancy: Early Aviation in Battersea and Wandsworth
Patrick Loobey
Recreation Department, Wandsworth Borough Council, 1981

The Wright Brothers were busy building aeroplanes in Battersea, South London, in the early 1900s. However, these were not the Wright Brothers, Wilbur and Orville, but two other Wright Brothers, Howard and Warwick, manufacturers of bespoke aircraft, including, in 1907, a helicopter for Frederico Capone of Naples. Tested on Norbury golf links, it achieved a maximum altitude of two feet.

Aeroplane Designing for Amateurs

Victor Lougheed

Chicago, IL: The Reilly & Britton Co., 1912

Unprotected Females in Norway; or, The Pleasantest Way of Travelling There

Emily Lowe

G. Routledge & Co., 1857

and:

Unprotected Females in Sicily, Calabria, and on the Top of Mount Etna

Routledge, Warnes & Co., 1859

The Glamour of Belfast

Hugh A. MacCarton

Dublin: Talbot Press, 1921

On Sledge and Horseback to Outcast Siberian Lepers

Kate Marsden

The Record Press, 1892

Sponsored by Dr Jaeger's Sanitary Woollen System Company Ltd., Wansborough's Nipple Shields and the Earlswood Asylum for Idiots and Imbeciles, Kate Marsden set off on her mission with a large quantity of supplies, including 40 lbs of plum pudding. She risked her life and health, fought off bears and wolves, and braved all manner of hardship during a 2,000-mile ride across Russia's icy wastes.

How
to
Abandon
Ship

Phil Richards   John J Banigan

SECOND EDITION

CORNELL MARITIME PRESS

The Little I Saw of Cuba
Burr McIntosh
F. Tennyson Neely, 1899

The 12C Bus: From Theory to Practice
Dominique Paret
Wiley, 1997

How to Abandon Ship
Philip Richards and John J. Banigan
New York: Cornell Maritime Press, 1942 (2nd edition)

'NOW with 40 more pages of NEW material.'

Build Your Own Titanic
Adam Rose
New York: Pedigree Books, 1981
Includes a folding iceberg tip.

Did Lewis Carroll Visit Llandudno?
Michael Senior
Llanrwst: Gwasg Carreg Gwalch, 2000

'An interesting exploration of the obscure evidence relating to a possible visit by Lewis Carroll to Llandudno, where he was inspired to write *Alice in Wonderland*. 25 black-and-white photographs.'
('Ymchwiliad diddorol i'r dystiolaeth aneglur ynglŷn ag ymweliad posibl gan Lewis Carroll â Llandudno, lle y cafodd ei ysbrydoli i ysgrifennu *Alice in Wonderland*. 25 ffotograff du-a-gwyn.')'

Nipponology Without Apology. A publication to further trade relations and goodwill between Great Britain and Japan
W. V. Simmons-Lynn
n.p., 1934–35

This book was published at a time when the principal exports from Britain to Japan included: 'tools, scientific instruments, electrical goods, machinery, cars, cycles' *and the principal imports into Britain from Japan were led by* 'tinned salmon, crab, mandarin oranges and pineapples'.

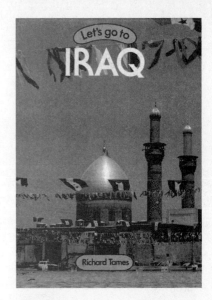

Let's Go to Iraq
Richard Tames
Franklin Watts, 1989

Teach Yourself to Fly
Nigel Tangye
English Universities Press, 1952

The Far East Comes Nearer
Hessell Tiltman
Jarrold, 1936

How to Avoid Huge Ships
John W. Trimmer
Centreville, MD: Cornell Maritime Press, 1993

Bridle Paths

Aimé Felix Tschiffely
Hodder & Stoughton, 1947

*The subtitle 'The story of a
ride through rural England'
and the claim that Mr Tschiffely
is pictured setting out on his
journey from the New Forest,
is somewhat belied by a cover
picture that appears to have been
photographed in Arizona.*

Yofuku; or, Japan in Trousers

Sherard Vines
Wishart & Co., 1931

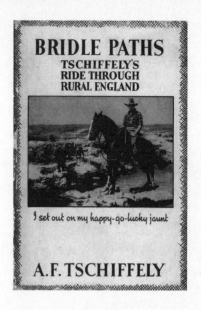

17

THE WORKPLACE

A Romance of Bureaucracy
'A–B'
Allahabad: A. H. Wheeler & Co., 1893

The Care of Raw Hide Drop Box Loom Pickers
Anon.
Saco, ME: Garland Manufacturing Co., 1922

Liver Building, Liverpool. List of Stop Cocks
Anon.
Toxteth: J. Litchfield (Printer), 1912

Tips on Tipping by Experienced Hands
Anon.
Frederick Warne, 1933

'Tipping one's own servants at Christmas is entirely a matter of taste. Quite 30% of British households do not tip them at all.'

The Joy of Cataloguing
Sanford Berman
Phoenix, AZ: The Oryx Press, 1981

The History of the Concrete Roofing Tile: Its Origin and Development in Germany
Charles Dobson
B. T. Batsford, 1959

'This book has been compiled with the single aim of interesting those who may like to learn something more about the origin and development of the concrete roofing tile than is generally known in England.'

THE HISTORY OF THE CONCRETE ROOFING TILE

Its Origin and Development in Germany

Charles Dobson

The Romance of Cement
Edison Portland Cement Company
*Providence, RI: Livermore & Knight
Co., 1926*

Law Relating to Carriage of Goods by Sea in a Nutshell
Marston Garsia
Sweet & Maxwell, 1923

In Love and Unity. A Book About Brushmaking
Thomas Girtin
Hutchinson, 1961

Control for Hotels & Restaurants
J. P. Guiney
Lamson Paragon Supply Co., 1913

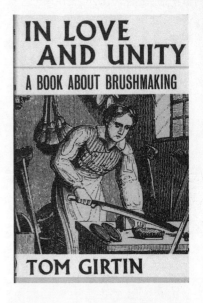

'The sole purpose of this book is to prevent irregularities, with all their evil consequences; to promote discipline among the staff, with consequent better service to patrons; and to ensure maximum profits at a minimum cost.'

Noise: Final Report
HMSO, 1964

Working with British Rail
Hugh Jenkins
Batsford, 1984

Dear Laughing Motorbyke [sic]: Letters from Women Welders of the Second World War
Margaretta Jolly (ed.)
Scarlet Press, 1997

How to Fire an Employee
Daniel T. Kingsley
Bicester: Facts on File, 1984

The Romance of the Civil Service
Samuel McKechnie
Samson Low, Marston & Co., 1930

The Time Registering Closet. A new system whereby much valuable time of employees is saved
Monitor Closet Company (Promotional booklet)
Warehouse Point, CT: Monitor Closet Co., 1892

'In these times of close competition and small profits it behoves the employer to get the best possible results from the labor of those in his employ in a legitimate way and at the same time study the comfort of the employee . . . Overseers of manufactories fully realize that much valuable time is "fooled" away by operatives absenting themselves from their places at frequent and unnecessarily long intervals to visit the Water Closet, and often a number are out at the same time, thus losing many *valuable minutes*, and in the aggregate *hours* of the employer's time. This notable abuse is obviated by the TIME REGISTERING CLOSET which completely and absolutely prevents an *enormous waste of valuable time with entire satisfaction* to both employer and employee.'

MANUFACTURERS' ATTENTION
— IS CALLED TO THE —
TIME REGISTERING CLOSET.
A NEW SYSTEM
Whereby Much Valuable Time of Employees is Saved.
LOOK. READ. INVESTIGATE.

70 Per Cent. of Time usually wasted is saved over Old System.

Investigation of the Monitor System Invited. "Time is Money." The Way to Make Money is to Save It.

Look at the above Cut.
Read the within Testimonials.
Investigate its Workings.

Romance of the Gas Industry

Oscar E. Norman
Chicago, IL: A. C. McClurg & Co., 1922

Proceedings of the Fifth Biennial Smut Workers Workshop

Mexico City: International Maize and Wheat Improvement Center, 1986

How To Avoid Work

William J. Reilly
Kingswood, Surrey; The World's Work (1913) Ltd., 1950

'Avoiding work is something which has fascinated me ever since I was a mere broth of a boy. In fact, I've made a profitable career out of avoiding work. And, as a professional career consultant, I've shown thousands of others how they can avoid work too.'

The History and Romance of Elastic Webbing Since the Dawn of Time

Clifford A. Richmond
Easthampton, MA: The Author, n.d.

The Elusive Art of Accounting

Howard Ross
New York: The Ronald Press, 1966

The Work being some episodes in the life of Charles Russell, as put forth in the papers left by him at Kijabi in the year of our Lord 1901

Printed for Private Circulation only at the Eweare Press (13 copies only); second edition (35 copies only).

The 'diary' of a Cockney boiler-maker working in Beira, Mozambique at the end of the nineteenth century. Liberally sprinkled with capital letters, rarely punctuated, and sodden with drink.

The Androgynous Manager

Alice Sargent
New York: Amacom, 1980

HOW TO AVOID WORK

By
William J. Reilly

If your job bores you — if it's work, not fun — it's hurting you. Get out of it! Here is a book that shows you:

1. How to move into a job you enjoy.

2. How to get the money you want with the greatest possible ease.

3. How to control your future from now on — with pleasure!

Wet Scrubbers
C. Schifftner & Howard E. Hesketh
John Wiley & Sons, 1986

True Screws Limited
'The Screw House', 1930

Grovelling & Other Vices: the sociology of sycophancy
Alphons Silbermann
New Brunswick, NJ.: Athlone Press, 2000

A Study of Telegraphists' Cramp
May Smith, Millais Culpin and Eric Farmer
Medical Research Council, Industrial Fatigue Research Board, HMSO, 1927

The Diseases of Electrical Machinery
George Wilfred Stubbings
E. & F. N. Spon, 1939

Keeping your Tools Tiptop
Thomas Umpleby
Detroit, MI: The Author, 1954

Careers in Dope
Dan Waldorf
Englewood Cliffs, NJ: Prentice Hall, 1973

Cleaning Up Coal
Gerhard Webber
New York: Harper & Row, 1982

Book-Keeping for Dentists
Frank 'Chalky' White
Baillière, Tindall & Cox, 1910

Credit for advice is also extended to Eustace B. L. White, and whiter-than-white accounts and teeth are guaranteed to all readers.

Music in the Typewriting Room
H. E. White
Sir Isaac Pitman, 1947

Umbrellas and parts of umbrellas (except handles). Report to the President on investigation no. TEA-I-6 under section 301(b)(1) of the Trade Expansion Act of 1962
Washington, DC: US Tariff Commission, 1964

The Infancy and Development of Linoleum Floorcloth
Frederick Walton
Simpkin, Marshall, Hamilton, Kent & Co., 1925

Passport to Survival: No. 1 How to Lose £30,000,000
Elijah Wilkes
Routledge & Kegan Paul, 1955

Described as 'A series of political pamphlets which analyse the evils from which our society is suffering today'. *Apparently this was the only one of the 12 titles in the series to be published.*

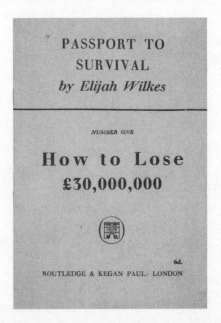

PASSPORT TO
SURVIVAL
by Elijah Wilkes

NUMBER ONE

How to Lose
£30,000,000

6d.
ROUTLEDGE & KEGAN PAUL: LONDON

18

CONFLICT: WARFARE & MARTIAL ARTS

Atomic Bombing: How to Protect Yourself
Watson Davis, et al.
New York: William H. Wise & Co., 1950

'Radioactivity is like a dog shaking itself after being in the water.'
　'Steaks are a must in the diet of the burn patient.'
　'American skyscrapers . . . are built on heavy steel frames.
Buildings such as these . . . would withstand the blast of an atomic
bomb.'
　'Curl up in a ball as you hit the ground.'

- If you are within 1,000 yards of the blast, what should you do
  immediately to minimize your danger?
- What types of clothing help protect your body against slow-
  killing ionizing rays?
- Where are the safest places to hide at home and away?
- How can you protect yourself from 'prompt' and 'lingering'
  radioactivity?
- How to protect yourself from burns and blindness.
- How can you decontaminate your family, pets, food and home of
  radioactivity?

How to Make an Atomic Bomb in your own Kitchen –
well, practically!
Bob Bale
New York: Frederick Fell, 1951

'Green Balls'. The Adventures of a Night Bomber
Paul Bewsher
Edinburgh: W. Blackwood & Sons, 1919

Gunrunning for Fun and Profit
Ragnar Benson
Boulder, CO: Paladin Press, 1986.

Aft – From the Hawsehole. Sixty-two Years of Sailors' Evolution
Lieutenant-Commander Henry D. Capper, O.B.E., R.N. (Late 'The Man Behind the Gun')
Faber & Gwyer, 1927

Tricks of Self-Defence ➤
W. H. Collingridge
Health and Strength, 1989

Fighting the Fuzzy-Wuzzy
E. A. De Cosson
John Murray, 1886

Hacking Through Belgium
Edmund Dane
Hodder & Stoughton, 1914
Dane was also the author of:

Trench Warfare: The Effects of Spade-Power in Modern Battles
United Newspapers, 1915

No. 20.

The Social History of the Machine Gun
John Ellis
New York: Pantheon Books, 1975

Catching a Cannon Ball
Walter Brown Gibson
St Louis, MO: n.p., 1923

War in Dollyland (A Book and a Game)
Harry Golding
Ward, Lock & Co., 1915
The battle between the Flat Heads and the Wooden Heads.

'The war fever is catching – awfully catching . . . The spy was led out at dawn . . . He died as a brave man should.'

Letty Hyde's Lovers: or, The Household Brigade
James Grant
Routledge, 1863

Nuclear War: What's In It For You?
Ground Zero War Foundation
New York: Pocket Books, 1982

Irish Swordsmen of France
Richard Francis Hayes
Dublin: M. H. Gill & Son, 1934

Warfare in the Enemy's Rear
O. Heilbrunn
Allen & Unwin, 1963

YOUR
ANSWER TO
INVASION –
JU-JITSU

UNARMED COMBAT

*The Art of Physical Defence and Attack
practically explained and illustrated by*

JAMES HIPKISS
(British Ju-Jitsu Champion)

INCLUDING A SPECIAL CONCISE COURSE FOR INSTRUCTORS

2/6

Your Answer to Invasion – Ju-Jitsu
James Hipkiss
F. W. Bridges, 1941

'With a knowledge of Unarmed Combat, even the unprepared citizens of Holland and Belgium could have frustrated the designs of Hitler's vital link in his plans – the Parachutists.'

'It should be realised that Unarmed Combat, or "Antagonistics", is as far in advance of Ju-Jitsu as the Tommy Gun is an improvement on the rifle.'

The 'Walking Stick' Method of Self-Defence
Herbert Gordon Lang
Athletic Publications, 1926

'In this little book there is offered a complete change of diet. To acquire proficiency in boxing, wrestling & Ju-Jitsu, demands . . . strenous effort and money. The Walking Stick method . . . demands none. The only appliance necessary is that possessed by nearly all; no special clothing or equipment is wanted; no, or little training,'

'Employ your SURPRISE PACKETS as speedily as you can' *and attack* '"soft spots" . . . Last, but by no means least, you must above all things impress on your opponent from the start your formidable qualifications . . . if you catch him, employ a means you have hitherto not been instructed in – your boot.'

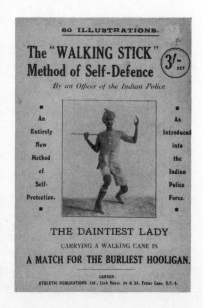

60 ILLUSTRATIONS.

The "WALKING STICK" Method of Self-Defence

3/- NET

By an Officer of the Indian Police

■ An Entirely New Method of Self-Protection. ■

■ As Introduced into the Indian Police Force. ■

THE DAINTIEST LADY
CARRYING A WALKING CANE IS
A MATCH FOR THE BURLIEST HOOLIGAN.

LONDON:
ATHLETIC PUBLICATIONS Ltd , Link House, 54 & 55, Fetter Lane, E.C. 4.

Nerves Versus Nazis

John Langdon-Davies
Routledge, 1940

'We need a manual of first aid for the mind . . . This is not a war of machines; it is a war of nerves. We must learn how to win the war of nerves . . . Noise is not dangerous: noise is the proof that the danger is over. Since I have lived to hear the bomb explode, I am safe from the bomb.'

Nuclear War Fun Book

Victor Langer & Walter Thomas
New York: Holt, Rinehart & Winston, 1983
'Nuclear War Games & Puzzles'

Nazi Nuggets

Clara Leiser
Victor Gollancz, 1939

Combat without Weapons

Capt. E. Hartley Leather
Aldershot: Gale & Polden, 1942

How to Live Calmly in War Time

'A London Journalist'
(Newman Watts)
Pickering & Inglis, 1940

A Do-It-Yourself Submachine Gun

Gerard Metral
Boulder, CO: Paladin Press, 1995

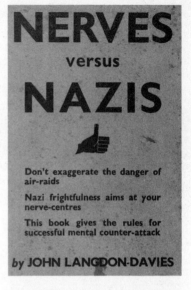

NERVES versus NAZIS

Don't exaggerate the danger of air-raids

Nazi frightfulness aims at your nerve-centres

This book gives the rules for successful mental counter-attack

by JOHN LANGDON-DAVIES

COMBAT WITHOUT WEAPONS by CAPT. E. HARTLEY LEATHER, R.C.A.

GALE & POLDEN LTD.

Price 1/6 net. by post 1/8

The Trapping and Destruction of Executive Armoured Cars

John A. Minnery
Cornville, AZ: Desert Publications, 1980

I Was a Kamikaze

Ryuji Nagatsuka
Abelard-Schuman, 1973

Hand Grenade Throwing as a College Sport

Lewis Omer
New York: A. G. Spalding & Bros, 1918

The British Library's copy has unfortunately been 'Destroyed by bombing'.

Defensive Tactics with Flashlights

John G. Peters Jr
Northbrook, IL: Calibre Press, 1983

'Hurrah!' A Bit of Loving Talk with Soldiers

Samuel Gillespie Prout
James Nisbet, 1881

Chapter IV: 'I'm going in for him – hard'.

Leadership Secrets of Attila the Hun

Wess Roberts
New York: Bantam Books, 1989

LEADERSHIP SECRETS OF ATTILA THE HUN

WESS ROBERTS PhD

'An imaginative and colourful approach to relating leadership principles that have long served those having the will to lead.'
Ken Blanchard, PhD, co-author of The One Minute Manager

Thrilling Experiences of the First British Woman Relieved by Lord Roberts
'By J. R.'
Aberdeen: Printed at the Aberdeen Journal Office. 1900

'Our Bobs is coming, our Bobs is coming!'

Thrilling Experiences

OF THE

First British Woman

RELIEVED BY

LORD ROBERTS.

BY J. R.

PRINTED AT THE ABERDEEN JOURNAL OFFICE.
1900.

The Sexual Cycle of Human Warfare
Norman Walter
Mitre Press, 1950

'. . . This book is dynamite . . . War stands in the same biological relationship to the vast organic body of society as sexual activity to the body of the individual . . . As we read these pages, we have a sense of rending veils, of shifting phantasmagoria, a presentiment that here at last we emerge upon a terrifying but epoch-making truth.'

The Secret Arts of Chinese Leg Manoeuvres in Pictures
Lee Ying-Arng
n.p., n.d.

'. . . the writer requests the reader to bear in mind that though by hitting the opponent's vital point is the most effective tactic in self-defence, it would incur calamity if executed recklessly . . . Unless it is most necessary, don't hit your opponent's vital point.'

THE SECRET ARTS OF
CHINESE LEG
MANOEUVRES
IN PICTURES

中國腿擊法

BY
LEE YING - ARNG

19

CRIME & THE LAW

The Development of a Procedure for Eliciting Information from Boys about the Nature and Extent of their Stealing
William Albert Belson, G. L. Millerson and P. J. Didcott
London School of Economics, 1968

Organizing Deviance
Joel Best and David F. Luckenbill
Englewood Cliffs, NJ: Prentice-Hall, 1982

Truncheons: Their Romance and Reality
Erland Fenn Clark
Herbert Jenkins, 1935
With over 100 plates illustrating more than 500 truncheons.

Having It Away. Thirteen Years of Crime
Leslie John Cunliffe
Duckworth, 1965

A Handbook on Hanging
Charles St Lawrence Duff
Cayme Press, 1928

Violence as Communication

Janny de Graaf and Alex Schmid

Beverly Hills, CA: Sage Publications, 1982

The Love Sonnets of a Hoodlum

Wallace Irwin

San Francisco, CA: Paul Elder, 1901

'Am I a turnip? On the strict
    Q.T.,
When do my Trilbys get so
    ossified?
Why am I minus when it's up to
    me
To brace my Paris Pansy for a
    glide?
Once more my hoodoo's thrown
    the game and scored
A flock of zeros on my tally-
    board.'

How to Pick Pockets. A Treatise on the Fundamental Principle, Theory and Practice of Picking Pockets

Eddie Joseph

The Vampire Press, 1946

Joseph was also the author of:

How To Do Cups and Balls

The Vampire Press, 1946

Forensic Examination of Rubber Stamps: A Practical Guide

Jan Seaman Kelly

Charles C. Thomas, 2002

CHRIST with the C.I.D.

Ex-Chief Inspector REGINALD MORRISH

Christ with the CID
Ex-Chief Inspector Reginald Morrish
Epworth Press, 1953

Cadaver Dog Handbook: Forensic Training and Tactics for the Recovery of Human Remains
Andrew Rebmann
Boca Raton, FL: CRC Press, 2000

Taking Life Imprisonment Seriously
Dirk van Zyl Smit
The Hague: Kluwer, 2002

The Bright Side of Prison Life
Captain S. A. Swiggett
Baltimore, MD: Fleet, McGinley & Co., 1897

On the Gallows
Violet Van der Elst
The Doge Press, 1937
Anti-hanging campaigner Van der Elst, also the author of
The Torture Chamber, *includes photographs of victims:*

'Haslam the Dwarf. Hanged at Manchester, February 24th, 1937 [*for battering a woman to death with a tyre lever*]. "One had only to look at those haunted eyes . . . seeming to foretell his doom."'

'Mrs Major, mother of three children. When she was hanged [*19 December 1934, for poisoning her husband*], her head was severed from her body.'

20

RELIGION & BELIEFS

The Love Letters of a Portuguese Nun
Marianna Alcoforado
Cassell, 1890

Female Tent Ritual
Anon.
Manchester: Independent Order of Rechabites, 1912

The Independent Order of Rechabites was a benefit society founded in 1835. The OED defines 'Rechabite' as 'one of a Jewish family descended from Jonadab, son of Rechab, which refused to drink wine or live in houses.'

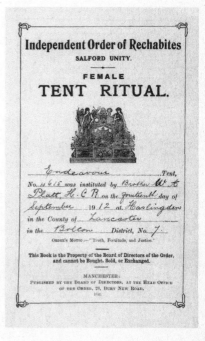

The Pious Christian's Daily Preparation for Death and Eternity . . . For The Use of Persons in Lingering Sickness or Under Sorrow and Affliction
Anon.
S.P.C.K., 1852

From Cleopatra to Christ. Arguing that the Former was the Latter's Mother

A. J. Bethell

The Author, 1921 (4 vols)

Typescript preserved in the British Library.

My Invisible Friend Explains the Bible

J. G. Bogusz

Boston, MA: Branden Press, 1971

Becoming a Sensuous Catechist

Therese Boucher

Mystic, CT: Twenty-Third Publications, 1984

So Your Wife Came Home Speaking in Tongues! So Did Mine!

Robert Branch

Old Tappan, NJ: Revel, 1973

Jesus In My Golf Cart

Bernita Jackson Brown, Paul Winer and Wanda Lund

Bloomington, IN: AuthorHouse, 2002

Cooking With God

Lori David and Robert L. Robb

Hollywood, CA: Ermine Publishers, 1978

'Cooking with God is truly a labor of love.'
(former First Lady Rosalyn Carter, quoted in the publisher's catalogue).

Remembrances of a Religio-Maniac

D. Davidson

Stratford-on-Avon: Shakespeare Press, 1912

God Drives a Flying Saucer. Astounding Biblical Revelations that prove the existence of UFOs and explain their spiritual significance to mankind

R. L. Dione
Corgi, 1973

Is God Amoeboid?

Rev. John W. Doherty
Ringwood: The Author, 1966

Did the Virgin Mary Live and Die in England?

Victor Dunstan
Cardiff: Megiddo Press, 1985

'In-depth research into the life and times of Jesus.

The Jesus family were WEALTHY people.

The disciples were all members of Jesus' family, or friends of the family and were . . . RICH . . .

Though Jesus was a Jew he was possibly of English descent . . . his grandmother born in Cornwall.

The Virgin Mary & Jesus DRANK ALCOHOL and attended parties . . .

The Virgin Mary's uncle was a RICH man . . . he had EXTENSIVE BUSINESS INTERESTS in Britain.

The Jesus family was closely interlinked with British Royalty.

The Virgin Mary gave birth to no less than seven children.'

Was Jesus Insane?

G. W. Foote
Progressive Publishing Co., 1891

Thirty-six Reasons for Believing in Everlasting Punishment

David Ponting Hendy
Marshall Bros., 1887

Walled Up Nuns and Nuns Walled In

Walter Lancelot Holland
Edinburgh: The Author, 1895

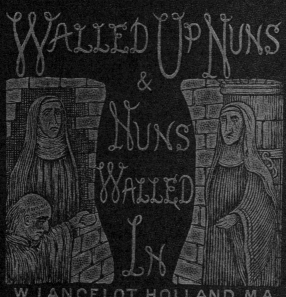

WALLED UP NUNS
&
NUNS
WALLED
IN

W. LANCELOT HOLLAND, M.A.

The Manliness of Christ
Thomas Hughes
Macmillan, 1879

Mathematical Principles of Theology; or, The Existence of God Geometrically Demonstrated
Richard Jack
C. Hawkins, 1745

The A, B, C Proverb: or, Pulpit at Home
George W. Johnson, Native African, Sierra Leone, late Secretary of the Egba Government, Abbeokuta. Entered at Stationers' Hall. I send you 2850 short sentences!! with: The Females' Guide, or Hand-book, how to use the No. 2 Creole Reversible, the first invention of our most worthy friend and countryman Mr George W. Johnson, Native African
n.p. [Liverpool], 1877

'The A, B, C Proverb, or Pulpit at Home, which I now venture to bring before my friends and the public, has been so long kept down in my mind, so much so, that when I begin to write each sentence, I was so full of words, both from dream, as well as by observation of the past, present and future matters, that I really do not know which and which to write down first . . .

The A, B, C boys and girls in the schools now-a-day, need know very learned philosopher of earth, to teach them through; and, with its two, – three, – and four simple letters joined together, such as, – "Do good, get good," "Do bad, get bad," is widely winning its way to the great end for which it was written . . .

I fall back to short sentences through the help of A, B, C, and burst my way through for your understanding, without reference (if you please) to Johnson's Dictionary, Webster's "Big Book" or Murray's Grammar . . .'

'58. A thing is lost when you cannot find it.

61. Arrange your house accordingly, and your house will be accordingly arranged.

93. A wife without love is a wife for everybody.

98. At the hour of death, refuse to drink medicine from Daddy M'Cray.

249. Black men must put shame aside in the streets of England, to push their way through.

348. Contrary to sweet will loose your bowels.

460. Dead bird cannot fly.

631. Elbow knocking among ladies, in the streets of England, gives the sign of a black-man in sight.

948. He who is in the habit of telling lies, must cease from eating crabs.

1466. It is time to make haste, when you are late.

1476. If everybody is marching to Hell, you would still be unsafe to be left behind.

1644. Kneel down to pray, and not to play.

1753. Love in a woman dies at no time, whilst that of a man needs a sharp looking after.

2294. Say No, when there is no Yes in your mouth.

2382. There is a groan in the bosom of the Africans against their white brothers, which I dare not say in this book.'

The 'Creole Reversible' *is a* 'most beautiful and famous design of Head Handkerchief . . . manufactured . . . under the sole management of Mr Johnson . . .'

Johnson's headwear, produced in Liverpool and exported to West Africa, led to his nickname of 'Reversible Johnson'. He was also known in England as 'Proverbial Johnson', or 'Prince Alfred' Johnson.

'. . . You asked me about England; that I tell you is a country not like Africa . . . in fact I find a great difference, so much so that I am unable to express myself for your understanding. This I know, that all are civilized – all busy and all seem to be doing well . . . It is a busy world where everybody is trying as hard as he can to get on – no long shaking of hands or long how-do-you-do in the streets by ladies and gentlemen; a nod as a compliment of the day is quite sufficient for them, which still makes quite a civilized people . . .'

Successful Fund-raising Sermons
Julius King
New York: Funk & Wagnalls, 1953

The Magic of Telephone Evangelism
Harold E. Metcalf
Atlanta, GA: Southern Union Conference, 1967

Traditional Aspects of Hell
James Mew
Swan Sonnenschein & Co., 1903

God's Gym: Divine Male Bodies in the Bible
Stephen D. Moore
Routledge, 1996

Would Christ Belong to a Labor Union? or, Henry Fielding's Dream
Rev. Cortland Myers
New York: Street & Smith, 1900

Masturbation in the American Catholic Church
Michael Stephen Patton
Ann Arbor, MI: University Microfilms International, 1984

Jesus in My Shoes
Lori Peckham and Tim Lale
Hagerstown, MD: Review and Herald Pub. Association, c.1998

Wrestlers with Christ
Karl Pfleger (translated by E. I. Watkin)
Sheed & Ward, 1936

Why There is Something rather than Nothing
Bede Rundle
Oxford: Oxford University Press, 2004

'While it is seemingly inconceivable that there should have been nothing at all, it is far from clear why there is what there is.'

Hell: Where Is It?
'Saladin' (pseudonym of W. Stewart Ross)
New Edition, W. Stewart and Co., c.1890

Ex-Nuns: a Study of Emergent Role Passage
Lucinda F. San Giovanni
Norwood, NJ: Ablex Publishing Corporation, 1978

Why Jesus Never Wrote a Book
William Edwin Robert Sangster
Epworth Press, 1932

Laughter at the Foot of the Cross
M. A. Screech
Boulder, CO: Westview Press, 1999

From the Monotremes to the Madonna. A Study of the Breast in Culture and Religion
Fabius Zachary Snoop
John Bale, Sons & Danielson, 1928

> 'The poet . . . takes the universe to be only an overwhelming maternity . . . perfecting the breast was Nature's supreme endeavour.'
> 'Curses and globular ellipses delight the eye as squares and parallelograms never do. Why does the sight of a ball afford more pleasure than a brick?'

The Fragrant Bosom of Aphrodite
The Bosom of the Father
Aaron's Breastplate
Mountains of Myrrh
The Bloody Teat
Vests

Beard Shaving, and the Common Use of the Razor, an Unnatural, Irrational, Unmanly, Ungodly and Fatal Fashion Among Christians
William Henry Henslowe
W. E. Painter, 1847

Electricity and Christianity
Crump J. Strickland
Charlotte, NC: Elizabeth Publishing, 1938

Five Years' Hell in a Country Parish
Rev. Edward Fitzgerald Synnott
Stanley Paul & Co., 1920

Synnott, the Rector of Rusper, accepted the living of Rusper in East Sussex, 'a sheltered rectory, over which the golden honeysuckle climbed. My flock were to be a few good-hearted rustics, who would greet their rector with a doff of the hat or an old-fashioned curtsey . . . The music of the birds would harmonise with my own care-free soul; for all would be joy and song within me . . .' *However* . . . 'I feel I must describe in all their terrible realism some of the agonising experiences through which I have passed . . . leading to the ruin of the rector and his family. After the most careful deliberation, I have decided to tell the whole world my remarkable story.'

Camp Prayers for Guides
Caroline Sheelagh Tatham
Girl Guides Association, 1948

Why Jesus was a Man and Not a Woman
Sydney Calhoun Tapp
Kansas City, MO: The Author, 1914

Dirty Laundry: 100 Days in a Zen Monastery
Robert Winson and Miriam Sagan
Albuquerque, NM: La Alameda Press, 1997

Eating the Baby Jesus
Enda Wyley
Dublin: Dedalus Press, 1993

21

DEATH

The Sunny Side of Bereavement
Rev. Charles Edwin Cooledge
Boston, MA: J. G. Cupples, 1890

Reusing Old Graves
Douglas Davies and Alastair Shaw
Shaw & Sons, 1995

Obituary Notices of Astronomers
Edwin Dunkin
Williams & Norgate, 1879

Sex After Death
B. J. Ferrell and Douglas Edward Frey
New York: Ashley Books, 1983

Deathing: an Intelligent Alternative for the Final Moments of Life
Anya Foos-Graber
Reading, MA: Addison-Wesley, 1984

Daddy Was an Undertaker
McDill McCown Gassman
New York: Vantage Press, 1952

The Art of Embalming
Thomas Greenhill
The Author, 1705

His mother, Elizabeth Greenhill (or Greenhille) is said to have had thirty-nine children.

LIVING

WITH THE

DEAD !

AN APPALLING POEM BY

A MADMAN.

ONE PENNY.

Buried Alive
Franz Hartmann
Boston, MA: Occult Publishing Co., 1895

Public Performances of the Dead
George Jacob Holyoake
London Book Store, 1865

Tell Me, Papa: Tell Me About Funerals
Marvin and Joy Johnson
Brooklyn, NY: Center for Thanatology Research and Education, 1980

Living with the Dead! An Appalling Poem
'A Madman' (Mark Wicks)
n.p., 1886

> **'A** man emerged from the hedge that bordered the ground of the institution. He was hatless – his cadaverous features of a ghastly hue . . . "A voice from the grave," said he; "A warning from the tomb – don't destroy it." . . . I give the papers just as I received them, word for word. A more appalling work I never read.**'**
> *Arthur Denclarvin, in the Introduction.*

Postmortem Collectibles
C. L. Miller
Atglen, PA: Schiffer Publishing, 2001

How I Know That the Dead Are Alive
Fanny Ruthven Paget
Washington, DC: Plenty Publishing Co., 1917

Do-it-yourself Coffins: For Pets and People
Dale L. Power
Atglen, PA: Schiffer Publishing, 1997
and:
Fancy Coffins To Make Yourself
Atglen, PA: Schiffer Publishing, 2001

Phone Calls from the Dead

D. Scott Rogo and Raymond Bayless

Englewood Cliffs, NJ: Prentice Hall, 1979

The Beginner's Guide for the Recently Deceased. A comprehensive guide to the only inevitable destination

David Staume

St Paul, MN: Llewellyn Publications, 2004

Premature Burial and How It May Be Prevented

William Tebb and Col. Edward Perry Vollum

Swan Sonnenschein & Co., 1896

The authors conclude that '. . . no evidence of death is really satisfactory except that which is supplied by putrefaction' *and suggest the building of what they describe as* 'waiting mortuaries . . . furnished with every appliance for resuscitation. Only when the fact of death has been unequivocally established by the sign of decomposition' *should the body be removed to the cemetery.*

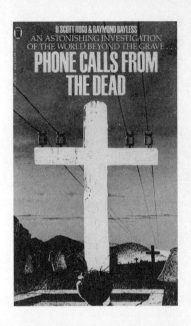

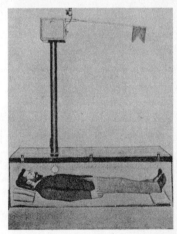

Do the Dead Ever Talk?
Edward Thurston
n.p., 1923

Yes:
The Dead Do Talk
John Bentley
Hutchinson, 1944

No:
The Dead Do Not Talk
Julien J. Proskauer
New York: Harper & Bros., 1946

Last Chance at Love
Various authors
New York, Pinnacle Books, 1981
The Terminal Romances *series.*

How to Conduct a One-day Conference on Death Education
Ellen Zinner and Joan McMahon
Brooklyn, NY: Center for Thanatology Research, 1980

JOKES CRACKED BY
LORD ABERDEEN

22

AGAINST ALL ODDS

The following books all found their way into print – somehow.

Jokes Cracked by Lord Aberdeen
Lord Aberdeen (John Campbell Gordon)
Dundee: Valentine, 1929

'In the realm of Wit and Humour, Lord Aberdeen is a name to conjure with. All the kindly geniality of the North comes out in his rich repertoire of stories, and here the Publishers have pleasure in introducing to a wider public a few Gems from his collection.'

There Must Be a Reason
Gilbert Anderson
Lewes: Guild, 1993

Marriage of Her Royal Highness the Princess Anne and Captain Mark Phillips. List of Wedding Presents. St James's Palace (with Addenda)
(Printed by Lund Humphries, 1973)

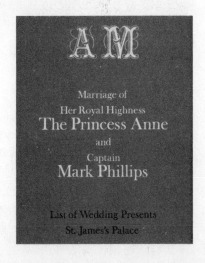

Almost 1,600 people gave presents, including:

Sodastream Ltd: A soda stream
Mr & Mrs Richard Parker-Bowles: Three green hippos
Sir Martin & Lady Chatteris: Two ornamental penguins
H.R.H. Princess Margaretha, Mrs John Ambler and Mr John Ambler:
   8 dozen coat hangers
Mrs Ada Barker and Mrs Alice Galagher: 3 coat hangers
Percy Edwards: Stainless steel tea strainer
Gerry Atkins: Tape of a hymn
Mrs E. E. Gott: Nine $2^1/2$p stamps
Miss Nasim Jafry: Bottle of scent – childs head as stopper
Miss Fiona Barr: Two swizzle sticks
Signor Mario Binda: A poem, *Anne*, by the donor
Mrs Matilda B. Kapicka: A packet of squash seeds
Masters Shaun & David Bradbury: A bulldog clip
Miss Grace Brown: Small glass mug with drummer on it
Miss M. E. A. Coleman: Sachet of shampoo
Miss Paul Kidd: Small stone
Miss S. Russo: Tablet of soap
Mrs V. Tyers: A poodle charm
Mr Seyfettin Tunc: Book, *O World Stop Revolving*, by the donor
Mr & Mrs J. Barratt: Sprig of myrtle
Master Mark Linder: A coin
Miss Angela Horsford: Two *Love is…* pillowcases
Miss Catherine Honlyk: Book, *Cooking for that Man*
Mrs J. G. Dean: A pottery badger
Rev. Canon and Mrs C. L. Conder: Three felt mice
Mr & Mrs Nicholas Kendal: Duster
Miss Alex Channer: Novelty handcuffs

Not a Success
Anon.
S.P.C.K., 1879

Octogenarian Teetotalers, with One Hundred and Thirteen Portraits
Anon.
National Temperance League Publication Depot, 1897

Bold Musings; being an attempt to create fundamental changes in public opinion and to help to emancipate thought from the thraldom of foolish time honoured tyrant customs; – written, out compliment to the subject, in lines of ten syllables, and in plain language. With an appendix of choice quotations.
By Anonymous
Printed not Published, 1870–71

A general index provides a list of 32 rejected titles, 'each one of which however would have described it'. *The shortest is* 'My Mind'. *The longest:* '*Eu*(not)*topos*(place), *alias* Utopia. Away with that Dog's bad name for falsely supposed impossible happiness – with that Satire on Providence! Small families, no marriages, no chastity, no *Cain-Abel*ism, *plus* some education, are the chief elements required to compose, not, nowhere but, every-where comfort.'

'This book has been printed by foreigners to the English language, on the Continent of Europe, and hence some errors of the press which are partly due, however, to my failing eyesight at reading distance . . . If this book ever becomes public, the author will not feel bound to answer any critics whom he may believe to be sufficiently answered by the authorities quoted by him or by his own logic.'

Not Worth Reading
Sir George Compton Archibald Arthur
Hutchinson & Co., 1914

The Incoherence of The Incoherence
Simon Van Den Bergh
Luzac & Co., 1954

Facing Retirement. A guide to the middle aged and elderly

'A Country Doctor'

George Allen & Unwin, 1960

Chapters include:

The Other Side of the Hill

Pensions

Wills

The Elderly Guest

Living Alone

Loneliness

Hard of Hearing

Painful Feet

Frosty but Kindly

Sweet Sleep. A Course of Reading Intended to Promote That Delightful Enjoyment

Charles J. Dunphie

Tinsley Brothers, 1879

Chapters include:

The Polite Arts of Yawning and Snoring

The Misery of Having One's Hair Cut

The Miseries of Development

The Pleasures of Poverty

On the Unimportance of Everything

The Delights of the English Climate

Pancakes

Banana Circus

Margaret Fisher and Henry Rox

Hammond Hammond Co., 1943

An entire circus troupe of bananas dressed as tightrope-walkers, clowns, jugglers, lion-tamers and banana animals. A surprising production, considering its date of publication, when bananas were virtually unobtainable in the UK.

BANANA
CIRCUS

Modelling and
Pictures by

HENRY
ROX

Told by
MARGARET
FISHER and
HENRY ROX

Blessed Be Drudgery
William Channing Gannett
British and Foreign Unitarian Association, 1890
'With a preface by the Countess of Aberdeen'.

Splay Feet Splashings
'Goosestep'
Leadenhall Press, 1891

Just Ordinary, But . . . An Autobiography
Joseph Halliday
Waltham Abbey: The Author, 1959

Poems in Praise of Practically Nothing
Samuel Hoffenstein
New York: Horace Liveright, 1928 (5 editions)
Includes: 'Poems intended to incite the utmost depression'

1587, a Year of No Significance
Ray Huang
New Haven, CT: Yale University Press, 1981

It's All About Me
Alvin Jackson Jr
Bloomington, IN: AuthorHouse, 2002

'The ultimate book of the century has finnaly [*sic*] arrived.'

Muddling Toward Frugality
Warren A. Johnson
San Francisco, CA: Sierra Club, 1978

Everybody's Lonesome
Clara Elizabeth Laughlin
New York: Fleming H. Revell, c.1910

The Human Side of Insurance
F. J. Maclean
Sampson Low, Marston, 1931

Is Life Worth Living?
William Hurrell Mallock
Chatto & Windus, 1882

Dumps; a Plain Girl
Elizabeth Thomasina Meade
W. & R. Chambers, 1905

Snoring as a Fine Art, and Twelve Other Essays
Albert Jay Nock
Freeport, NY: Books for Libraries Press, 1958

The Wit of Prince Philip
H.R.H. Prince Philip
Leslie Frewin, 1965

It's a Wog's Life. By Golly.
Sidney Samuel Theodore Rowe
Hanley: Privately printed for the author by Webberley Ltd., 1966

The reminiscences of a 'Hindu Aryan'. Chapters include:

Let Sleeping Wogs Lie
Watch Wog
Barking Wogs
Give a Wog a Bone
Cats and Wogs
Mad Wogs and Englishmen
In the Wog House

250 Times I Saw a Play

Keith Odo Newman

Oxford: Pelagos Press, 1944

The author fails to mention what the play was, who wrote it, where it was performed and who acted in it. George Bernard Shaw commented:

> 'I don't know what to say about this book. The experience on which it is founded is so extraordinary, that an honest record of it should be preserved . . . But it would have driven me mad; and I am not sure that the author came out of it without a slight derangement.'

Little-Known Sisters of Well-Known Men

Sarah J. Pomeroy

Boston, MA: Dana Estes, 1912

Eight Years of His Life a Blank. The Story of Pioneer Days in South Dakota

Levi Judson Ross

Waterton, S D: W. R. Lambert, c.1915

The Meaning of Unintelligibility in Modern Art

Edward Francis Rothschild

Chicago, IL: University of Chicago Press, 1934

The Musings of a Martian

'Sea-Pup'

Heath Cranton Ltd., Fleet Street, 1920

Short essays by an alienated man constantly on the sick list.

> 'Of literary talent I have none [but] I can claim to have had an almost unique experience of naval, military and Ministry of Pensions hospitals . . . When I entered hospital I was a boy . . . I have emerged from hospital life to find a new manhood . . .'

With the
facsimile of a comment by Bernard
Shaw

250
Times
I saw
a Play

by
K·O·NEWMAN

Golden Quotations of Our First Lady
Julio F. Silvero
Caloocan City, Philippines: National Book Store, 1978
An anthology of 300 quotations from Imelda Marcos.

The Romance of Colonization
George Barnett Smith
S. W. Partridge, 1897

A Chapter in Mediocrity
William James Stavert
Skipton: Craven Herald Office, 1896
The author was Rector of Burnsall, Yorkshire.

Along Wit's Trail: the Humor and Wisdom of Ronald Reagan
L. William Troxler
New York: Owl Books, 1984

'He has been called the funniest president since Lincoln.'

My Tablecloths
Ethel Brilliana Tweedie
Hutchinson, 1916

The Darjeeling Disaster – Its Bright Side
Francis Wesley Warne
Calcutta: The Methodist Publishing House, 1900

How to Be Happy though Human
W. Béran Wolfe
George Routledge, 1932

BIBLIOGRAPHY: THE REFERENCE SECTION

Bibliography of Mangrove Research, 1600–1975
Anon.
Paris: UNESCO, 1981

How To Do It; or, Directions for Knowing or Doing Everything Needful
Anon.
New York: J. F. Tingley, 1864

Supplement to Complete Book of Ballet
Cyril W. Beaumont
The Author, 1942

Indexers & Indexes in Fact & Fiction
Hazel K. Bell (ed.)
Toronto: Toronto University Press, 2001

Contains some unusual examples:
Adultery, insufferable, by anyone not of royal blood . . .
Affection, immoderate, for our own work, cure of, *see* Pulping
Alarm, no cause for on *Titanic*
Anybody, mere page-numbers not of the slightest use to
Chastity, *see* Homicide
Chaucer, appalling spelling of
Fun, no authority for the idea that we are here for
Heaven, system of book-keeping in use in
Marriage, not, legally, the same as slavery
Nouvelle cuisine, contrasted with food
Split personality, held, does not excuse bigamy
Wet nurses, male parents useless as
Weisskreuz Hotel, its manager well worth making love to

A Selected Bibliography of Snoring or Sonorous Breathing

Marcus H. Boulware

Nashville, TN: Sonorous Breathing Research Project, Tennessee State A and I University, 1967

The Penis Inserts of Southeast Asia: An Annotated Bibliography with an Overview and Comparative Perspectives

Donald E. Brown, James W. Edwards, and Ruth Moore

Berkeley, CA: Center for South and Southeast Asia Studies, 1988

Specifications for Billets for Picking Sticks for Underpick Looms

British Standards Institution

BSI, 1965

A Register of Royal and Baronial Domestic Minstrels, 1272–1327

Constance Bullock-Davies

Boydell, 1986

Barbs, Prongs, Points, Prickers, and Stickers: A Complete and Illustrated Catalogue of Antique Barbed Wire

Robert T. Clifton

Norman, OK: University of Oklahoma Press, 1970

Encyclopedia of Pocket Knives

Roy Ehrhardt

Kansas City, MO: Heart of America Press, (3 vols.), n.d.

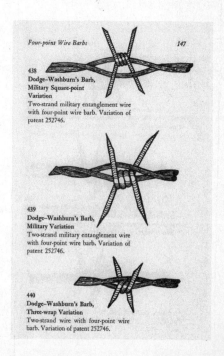

Four-point Wire Barbs 147

438
Dodge–Washburn's Barb,
Military Square-point
Variation
Two-strand military entanglement wire
with four-point wire barb. Variation of
patent 252746.

439
Dodge–Washburn's Barb,
Military Variation
Two-strand military entanglement wire
with four-point wire barb. Variation of
patent 252746.

440
Dodge–Washburn's Barb,
Three-wrap Variation
Two-strand wire with four-point wire
barb. Variation of patent 252746.

Barbs, Prongs, Points, Prickers, & Stickers

A Complete and Illustrated
Catalogue of Antique
Barbed Wire

Robert T. Clifton

A Compendium of the Biographical Literature on Deceased Entomologists
Pamela Gilbert
British Museum (Natural History), 1977

Multi-Armed Bandit Allocation Indices
John C. Gittins
Chichester: Wiley, 1989

The Cruising Association Library Catalogue
Herbert James Hanson
Cruising Association, 1927

Biographical Dictionary of Irishmen in France
Richard Francis Hayes
Dublin: M. H. Gill & Son, 1949

Encyclopedia of Shampoo Ingredients
Anthony L. L. Hunting
Cranford, NJ, 1983; Weymouth, 1991

A Catalogue of Swedish Local Postage Stamps, issued from 1941 to 1947
Raymond George Lister
Dumfries: K. Jahr, 1952

An Annotated Bibliography of Evaporation
Grace J. Livingston
Washington, DC: Weather Bureau, 1910

Lobbery. 20,000 Lobbs around the world. Vol. I.
Douglas H. V. Lobb
Truro: The Author, 1992

Lights! Catalogue of Worldwide Matchbox Labels with the Word 'Light' in the Title
Raymond W. Norris
Royston: British Matchbox Label and Booklet Society, 1983

Railway Literature, 1556–1830
Robert Alexander Peddie
Grafton & Co., 1931

The Encyclopedia of Alcoholism
Robert O'Brien and Morris Chafetz
Bicester: Facts on File, 1983

Biographical Dictionary of Wax Modellers
Edward Pyke
Oxford: Oxford University Press (Vol. 1), 1973;
The Author (Vols. 2 and 3), 1983

A Million Random Digits
Rand Corporation
Glencoe, IL: The Free Press, 1955

> 'The random digits in this book were produced by rerandomization of a basic table generated by an electronic roulette wheel.'

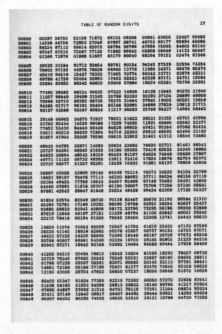

A Dictionary of International Slurs
A. A. Roback
Cambridge, MA: Sci-Art Publishers, 1944

Bibliography of the Rhinoceros
L. C. Rookmaaker
Rotterdam: A. A. Balkema, 1983

List of Persons Whose Names Have Been Changed in Massachusetts 1780–1883
Boston, MA: Secretary of the Commonwealth, 1884

Selective Bibliography of the Literature of Lubrication
Nathan Van Patten and Grace S. Lewis
Kingston, Ont.: N. Van Patten, 1926

1001 Things You Can Get Free
Mort Weisinger
New York: Bantam, 1957

'A Fabulous New Treasury of America's Choisest Giveaway Items.'

'Ever envy the way the heroes in Hollywood films achieve that well-groomed look by the perfect way they knot their tie? It's easy to obtain the same effect, if you know how. For an illustrated brochure on how to tie a better knot, send for 'Tie Lore Booklet' . . .

'Free movie to show in your own home: "Lifeline". Action picture which stars famous actor Thomas Mitchell and tells the exciting story of rope and twine.'

The Illustrated Encyclopedia of Metal Lunch Boxes
Allen Woodall and Sean Brickell
Atglen, PA: Schiffer Publications, 1997

REMARKABLE NAMES
OF REAL AUTHORS

A

W. Anker

Pierre Anus

Istvan Apathy

B

Gaspar Griswold Bacon

Pierre Jean Jacques Bacon-Tacon

Nellie Badcock

Thomas Baddy

Ole Bagger

Marmaduke Baglehole

Ludwig von Baldass

R. C. Balls

Paula Balls-Organista

Melville Balsillie

Author of *Let's Enjoy Ourselves*,
The Cadet Supply Association,
1960

Jean Baptiste Banal

Yoshimoto Banana

Rebecca Hammering Bang

Otto Banga

Author of *Main Types of the
Western Carotene Carrot and
Their Origin*, Zwolle: W. E. J.
Tjeenk Willink, 1963

Gay Esty Bangs

Ida Barney

Marston Bates

Author of *Man in Nature*,
Englewood Cliff, NJ: Prentice
Hall, 1961, and *Gluttons and
Libertines: Human Problems of
being Natural*, New York: Vintage
Books, 1971

Jerry Belch

Krista Bendová

Author of *Cacky-hracky*
Bratislava: Mladé Letá, 1958

Rudyard Kipling Bent

Arngrim Berserk

Pseudonym of Olof Von Dalin

Myrtle Berry

Nicolas Bidet

John Thomas Bigge

Juana Bignozzi

René Palaprat de Bigot

Petr Bitsilli

Hippolyte Blot

Johanna Blows

Mody Coggin Boatright

Co-author, with James F. Dobie, of
Straight Texas, Austin, TX: Folk
Lore Society of Texas, 1937

Ion Bog

A. Bogie

Bishop Boguphalus II

Don Bolognese
Johannes Bogusz
Margot Bollock
Hugo Bonk
Don Bonker
Twat Booth
Celina LuZanne Boozer
Omen Konn Boring
Nancy Boy
    Full name: Nancy Hess Omaha Boy
Wallop Brabazon
Melt Brink
Malte Brunk
Aage Bugge
Hildegard Bung
Al Burt
Reynaldo Kuntz Busch

C

Perin H. Cabinetmaker
Desiré Carnel
Albert Chop
Eva Choung-Fux
A. Clot
    Full name: Antoine Barthélemi Clot
Harry Cock
Paul Condom
Ellsworth Prouty Conkle
    Author of *Crick Bottom Plays*,
    1928, *Poor Old Bongo*, 1954 and
    Son-of-a-Biscuit-Eater, 1958, all
    published in New York by Samuel
    French
Clement Crock
Cornelius Crocus
Lettice May Crump
Mari Anus Cuming
    Author of *The Drummer Boy*,
    Detroit, 1868

D

Richard L. Daft
    Author of *Understanding
    Management*, 1998
Eugeniusz Dalek
Dee Day
T. Fox Decent
Mayhew Derryberry
Roger A. Destroyer
Robert Baby Buntin Dicebat
    His collected poems were
    published under the title
    Superman, Constable, 1934
Hugh Dick
Arsen Diklíc
Kersi D. Doodha
Ben Dover

E

Knud Eel
Gottfried Egg
Gordon Bandy Enders

F

Achilles Fang
Vera Fartash
A. Farto
Paul Fatout
Léonce Ferret
Francis M. Fillerup
Gottfried Finger
Stuyvesant Fish
Hans Flasche
Mercedes Fórmica
Bishop Edmund Freke
Ernst Friedegg
V. B. Frog
Jessie Peabody Frothingham
Semen Frug

Mingyi Fucha
Stanka Fuckar
Martin Fucker
Diego Fucks
Clothilde Embree Funk
László Fussy
Brigitte Fux

G
Gergely Gergely
Bess Goodykoontz
Biserka Grabar
B. Noice Grainger
George L. Grassmuck
Wolf-Dietrich Grope
Jānis Grots
Manfred Grunt
Romulus Guga
Serge Gut

H
Bernard Haggis
Archibald Swiney Haig
Frederick Stuft Hammer
Billings Learned Hand
Odd Bang Hansen
O. Heck
Ottiwell Heginbothom
O. Hell
Burt Heywang
    Author of *Poultry Management
    in Subtropical, Semiarid Climates,*
    Washington, DC: United States
    Department of Agriculture, 1937
J. Hogsflesh
Frederik Winkel Horn
Hugo Horny
Henry Hornyold-Strickland
Stephen Herbert Wynne Hughes-Games

Herbert Hunger

I
Albert Irk

J
John Thomas Jeffcock

K
Kah-Ge-Ga-Gah-Bowh *aka* George
    Copway
Ivan Kandyba
Jup Kastrati
Lieselotte Kattwinkel
Solon Toothaker Kimball
Kurt Kink
Joseph Kinky
A. Kipper
Per Klang
Jèurgen Klapprott
Claudia Klodt
Onno Klopp
Hieronimus Knicker
Verona Butzer Knisely
Bent Koch
    Author of *Coryphoid Palm Fruits
    and Seeds from the Danian of
    Nāugssauq, West Greenland,*
    1972
K. Kong
Thorgny Ossian Bolivar Napoleon
    Krok
Erno Kunt

L
Joy Muchmore Lacey
    Author of *Jiggers, A Dog Story,*
    Chicago: Rand McNally, 1942
Dirk La Cock

Roger Laprune
Moses Lard
Faith B. Lasher
Hyacinthe Joseph Alexandre Thabaud de Latouche
Bishop Spencer Stottesbery Gwatkin Leeson
F. Leflufy
Julius Lips
V. Livshits-Filinsky
Tit Wing Lo
Roberto Jorge Haddock Lobo
Norbert Lohfink
P. van Loo
Barbara Lube
Bishop Lucifer of Cagliari
Georg Lunge
    Co-author with Ferdinand Hurter
Manfred Lurker

M
Agogo Mago
Pilgrim Mangles
Henry Manure
Sue Mee
Alf Roar Dag Meyerhöffer
Robert Duguid Forrest Pring Mill
Miriam Minger
Maximilian Mintz
Voltaire Molesworth
George Wigram Pocklington Money
Simon Young-Suck Moon
Professor A. Moron
John A. Morose
Rocco L. Motto
John Muckarsie

N
Hans Regina Nack

Bishop Frediricus Nausea
Endel Nirk
C. B. Noisy
Herbert Roof Northrup
Santiago I. Nudelman
Mildred Moody Nutter

O
Jacques Off
Bishop Henry Ustick Onderdonk
Violet Organ
Georg Ostrich

P
P. C. Pant
Jean Claude Pecker
Else Pée
Emmanuel Perve
William Piddle
Thomas Strangeways Pigg-Strangeways
Polycarpe Poncelet
Mu-chou Poo
Ismo Porn
Willy Prick
Willibald Psychyrembel
Ruth Rice Puffer
Harold Herman Punke
Mme J. J. Fouqueau de Pussy
Walter Lytle Pyle
    Author of *A Manual of Personal Hygiene*, etc.

Q
Marinus Lambertus Quack
Willem Quackelbeen

R
Maurice Rat

Camillo Ravioli
Hugh Ray
Hans Rectanus
Curt Redslob
Edna Risque
Valve Ristok
Margaret Cool Root
Fritz Rotter
Harry Rump

S
Flora Schmalz
Johann von Schmuck
Adriaen van Schrieck
A. Schytte
Doris Pogue Screws
Peter M. Semen
Timothy J. F. Sex
    Author of *Coastwise Cruising*,
    Lymington: The Nautical
    Publishing Co., 1970
Abraham Shag
Theodore Shite
I. I. Shitts
I. M. Sick
Mrs Hepsa Ely Silliman
Count Jacques de Silly
Louis Sinner
Isidore Snapper
Ivor Snook
Ku Sok-pong
James Spider
    Author of *How to Prevent Hog
    Cholera*, 1889
Sandie Spleen
Wolfgang Sucker

T
Negley King Teeters
Morten Thing
Jacques Tits
    Author of *Moufang Polygons*,
    2002
Nit Tongospit
Wade Toole
André Tosser

V
E. G. Vagina
Anna Ethel Twitt De Vere
Zenobia N. Vole

W
Rolf Wank
William Wanker
Lisa H. Weasel
James Weird
Urban Grosskipper von Wipper
    Compiler of *Cassell's English-
    Dutch, Dutch-English Dictionary*,
    Cassell and Co., 1951
Walter Womble
Ole Worm
Matilda Wrench
Sabina Wurmbrand

Y
Yury Yuriiovich Yurk

Z
Vittorio Zoppi

ACKNOWLEDGEMENTS

Fiammetta Alley; Steve Archer; Alfred Armstrong; Caroline Ash; Philip Athill; Atlantis; Richard Axe; Michael Baker; Robert Baldock; M. & M. Baldwin; Lionel Barnard; Louis Baum; Robin de Beaumont; Gail Benjafield; Nick Bernstein; *The Bookdealer*; *The Bookseller*; Nancy Boothe; Simon Brett; British Library; Stuart Broad; Stan Brown; A. J. Browning; Derek Bryant; Mark Bryant; Karen Bullock; Nigel Burwood; Iain Campbell; Mark Campbell; Bill Carrick; Peter Carter; Pat Cassidy; Philip Chancellor; M. & B. Clapham; Stephen Clarke; Laurie Cohen; Richard Constable; Graham Cornish; Countryside Books; John H. Cranwell; James Cummins; Michael D'Autreau; Richard Dalby; Paul Davies; Patrick Davis; David Dawson; David Daymond; Rebecca Dearman; Mark deVoto; The Diagram Group; Paul Dickson; Disley Bookshop; Prof. David Downes; Andrew Duckworth; Roy Eden; John Eggeling; Christopher Eley; Toby English; Len Evans; Evrah Evrah; Ray Feather; Sylvia Fenlon; David Fielder; David Flint; James Flynn; Tony Fothergill; Camilla Francombe; Laurie E. Gage; Patrick Gallagher; Joseph L. Gardner; Malcolm Gerratt; David Gillham; Mike & Sue Goldmark; Mike Goodenough; William Goodsir; Grandfather from Hell; A. Micallef Grimaud; Liz Groves; William Gummer; E. Hallett; Lionel Halter; Sylvia Hamilton; Gail Harbour; Dave Harris; George G. Harris; William Hartston; David Haxby; Tim Healey; Chris Heppa; Bernard Higton; Bevis Hillier; Geoff Hinchcliffe; David Holmes; Philip M. Hopper; Horsham Bookshop; D. F. Howard; Philip Howard; Jolyon Hudson; Spike Hughes; Barry Humphries; Kathy Hunnicutt; Mary Hutchinson; Paul Hutchinson; Betty Hyde; Paul Raymond Hyde-Lee; C. Hyland; Chris Irwin; Ian Jackson; D. Jarvis; Pete Jermy; Christopher Johnson; Annette Jolly; Richard Glyn Jones; Martin Keene; George Kelsale; Keith Kenyon-Thompson; Bryan Kernaghan; Sarah Key; Miles Kington; John Kinnane; Michele Kohler; Patty Lafferty; Edward

Nassau Lake; Adam Langley; Robert Larmour; *Library Journal;* Raymond Lister; George Locke; John A. Lord; Loughborough Bookshop; John Lyle; Ian Lynn; Julian Mackenzie; D. H. Mader; Maggs Bros.; Vivian T. Maisey; Jo Manning; Nell McCorry; R. McCutcheon; I. McDowell; Andrew McGeachin; Collin McLeod; Rod Mead; S. P. Milanytch; Peter Miller; Ian Miller; John Miller; Brian Mills; Montpelier Books; Michael Moon; C. R. Moore; Charles Mortimer; G. Mosdell; Carol Murphy; Margaret Nangle; Janet Nassau; New York Public Library; Kent Nielsen; Angus O'Neill; Michael Parsons; The PBFA; C. J. Phillips; John Phillips; Roy Pitches; Michael Powell; Primrose Hill Books; The Printer's Devil; Michael Prowse; John Randall; Ann M. Ridler; Mark Rogers; John D. Roles; Adrian Room; Prof. Robert Rosenthal; Theo Rowland-Entwistle; Ruth Royce; Robert Rubin; Christine A. Ruggere; Matthew Searle; Tony Seaton; Barry Shaw; Brian Shawcross; M. Shearer; Peter Shellard; Alan Shelley; Leslie Shepard; Leslie Sherlock; Stanley Shoop; Paul Sieveking; Louis Simmonds; Mrs M. I. Simpson; Ronald K. Smeltzer; Frank Smith; H. Smith of Liverpool Library; Harold Smith; Helen Smith; Timothy D'Arch Smith; Richard Spafford; I. G. Sparkes; D. Spector; Stewart Spencer; J. R. Sperr; David Stagg; Brian Staples; Peter Stavert; Martin Steenson; Andrew Stewart; Colin Stillwell; Christine Stockwell; G. E. C. & R. N. Stone; Martin Stone; Neil Summersgill; Mitchell Symons; Nigel Tattersfield; Phil Thredder; Karen Thomson; Brian Tomes; Jeff Towns; M. Treloar; Triangle; Christine Trollope; Nicholas Tucker; Dr R. J. Tunbridge; Morris Venables; Judi Vernau; Philip Walker; David Wallechinsky; John Walton; Philip Ward; David Watkin; Susan Watkin; Steve Weissman; Robert Weissner; Bruce Whiteman; Anabelle Whittet; Avril Whittle; Nicholas Willmott; Alan Wilson; Philip Wilson; Gerry Wolstenholme; Charles B. Wood III; Les Wray; Robin Wright; Vivian Wright; Stephen Wycherley; Michael Zinman

. . . and our apologies to anyone inadvertently omitted.

BIZARRE INDEX

Page numbers in bold indicate full-page illustrations